# Taking Your Customer Care™
## To the Next Level

# TAKING YOUR CUSTOMER CARE™ TO THE NEXT LEVEL

## Customer Retention Depends Upon Customer Care™

Nadji Tehrani and Steve Brubaker

authorHOUSE®

*AuthorHouse*™
*1663 Liberty Drive*
*Bloomington, IN 47403*
*www.authorhouse.com*
*Phone: 1 (800) 839-8640*

© 2015 Nadji Tehrani and Steve Brubaker. All rights reserved.

No part of this book may be reproduced, stored in a retrieval system, or transmitted by any means without the written permission of the author.

Published by AuthorHouse    08/27/2015

ISBN: 978-1-5049-3302-5 (sc)
ISBN: 978-1-5049-3303-2 (hc)
ISBN: 978-1-5049-3304-9 (e)

Library of Congress Control Number: 2015913735

Print information available on the last page.

Any people depicted in stock imagery provided by Thinkstock are models, and such images are being used for illustrative purposes only. Certain stock imagery © Thinkstock.

This book is printed on acid-free paper.

Because of the dynamic nature of the Internet, any web addresses or links contained in this book may have changed since publication and may no longer be valid. The views expressed in this work are solely those of the author and do not necessarily reflect the views of the publisher, and the publisher hereby disclaims any responsibility for them.

To my dear wife Juliette, my son Richard and his wife Mariana, my daughter Michelle and her husband David, my grandchildren Priscilla, Nicole, Isabella and Dylan. Thank you for your support and loving kindness.

Nadji Tehrani

To my wife Robin, daughters Elise and Elizabeth and my parents Bob and Juanita, who always provide me with great inspiration. Thank you for giving each day of my life a greater purpose.

Steve Brubaker

# Contents

Acknowledgements: ................................................................... ix
Foreword by Rich Tehrani: ....................................................... xi
Introduction: .......................................................................... xv

Chapter One:        Customer Satisfaction Is Not Enough:
                    You Must Go the Extra Mile ................... 1

Chapter Two:        Taking Care of Your Customers Takes
                    Care of Your Business ............................. 11

Chapter Three:      Marketing Defined in the Age of
                    Automation .............................................. 37

Chapter Four:       Business Is Personal: One to One
                    Marketing Leads to Customer
                    Engagement and Retention ................... 49

Chapter Five:       The Careful Treatment of Customers
                    Results in Customer Retention ............. 59

Chapter Six:        Don't Lead from Behind: Leadership
                    Empowers Your Team to Deliver Next
                    Level Customer Care™ ........................... 81

Chapter Seven:      Teach Employees to Care...Train, Train
                    and Retrain: The Customer is Always Right ... 91

Chapter Eight:      Listen and Learn: Gain a Complete
                    View of Your Customers ...................... 101

Chapter Nine:       The Principles for Taking Your
                    Customer Care™ to the Next Level ..... 117

| | | |
|---|---|---|
| Chapter Ten: | Meeting the Needs of Mobile Customers | 125 |
| Chapter Eleven: | Social Media and the Public Airing of Customer Grievances | 143 |
| Chapter Twelve: | What Goes Around Comes Around... Next Level Customer Care™: Reputation Management and Competitive Advantage | 159 |
| Summary: | The Skill that Delivers Awesome Customer Care™: Taking Responsibility | 185 |
| Book Preview: | Announcing the Important Follow-Up Book by the same authors: Taking Your Marketing Strategy to the Next Level™ | 189 |
| About the Authors: | Nadji Tehrani | 193 |
| | Steve Brubaker | 198 |
| Appendix: | The Ritz-Carlton Gold Standards | 201 |
| | The Gary L. and Karen S. Taylor Institute for Direct Marketing | 205 |

## Acknowledgements:

Nadji and I met at TMC's first Customer Care™ trade show, TBT 1986, in Atlanta. I had only been with InfoCision for one year, so the chance to see the incredible industry we were a part of was captivating. Nadji is a founding father of the industry, and I was eager to learn from him and gain insight that played a significant role in beginning my career. In the decades since, we've continued to work together, and as a result I'm happy to say we have become good friends.

The decision to create this book came from a discussion between Nadji and me on a beautiful sunny afternoon in Miami Beach this past February. I had always wanted to write a book and when I told Nadji my goal, he immediately offered to partner with me and put our years of experience together. This was an incredible and life changing offer for me as Nadji is one of the most well-respected and influential leaders in the world of communications...if you want to verify that fact, simply Google his name.

We both knew the concepts of Customer Care™ are an area of critical importance in business today. Companies spend millions of dollars bringing on new customers, but then all too often allow them to leave for a competitor due to neglect or misunderstanding. We also realized from our personal experiences that we were not being treated with proper Customer Care™ in many of our personal business relationships.

*Nadji Tehrani; Steve Brubaker*

By making customer retention a top priority through the principles of *Next Level Customer Care*™ outlined in this book, businesses will significantly improve their profitability and success.

There have been numerous people who have contributed in the process of completing this book and we must express our gratitude. Nadji and I offer sincere thanks to each one of you for your support:

- Rich Tehrani, CEO and group editor-in-chief at TMC. Rich provided insightful consultation as well as the Foreword to this book.
- Paula Bernier, executive editor at TMC
- Alan Urkawich, associate vice president of creative at TMC
- Carrie Majewski, director of content marketing, Content Boost
- Chhityz Thapa, senior web director at TMC
- Diana Stein, social marketing manager at TMC
- Dr. Dale Lewison, retired marketing department chair of twenty-eight years and executive director of The Taylor Institute for Direct Marketing at The University of Akron, as well as the author of <u>Retailing</u> textbook.
- Dr. Andrew Thomas, associate professor of marketing and international business at The University of Akron, and *New York Times* best-selling author.

Finally, I want to thank Gary, Karen and Craig Taylor, owners of InfoCision who have been so incredibly supportive over the past 30 years. Although Gary is no longer with us on this earth, he was an incredible mentor to me and I will always remember him with great respect and admiration.

Steve Brubaker

# Foreword by Rich Tehrani:
## CEO of Technology Marketing Corp.
### www.tmcnet.com

Next Level Customer Care™ is more relevant today than ever before. In 2001, I introduced what I called 'Tehrani's Law of Customer Service.' Here is what I said then in <u>INTERNET TELEPHONY</u> magazine published by our company Technology Marketing Corp.:

"I would like to propose a new theory on customer service in this age of the new economy. Almost everyone on the customer interaction front lines has heard the rule that,

**"it is 10 times more expensive to attract a new customer than it is to keep an existing one."**

But this rule was made before the Internet took off and certainly doesn't take into account websites like sucks.com where the world can complain about any company and the rest of the world can instantaneously read about it and respond. Consequently, I feel this rule needs to be brought into the 21$^{st}$ century, where websites, chat rooms and email..."

*(I said this before Facebook and Twitter took off, let alone the rest of the social media platforms)...*

"...allow customer opinions to spread more rapidly than ever before, I would like to call this new rule:

## Tehrani's Law of Customer Service 2015:
**"In the Internet era, it is 100 times more expensive to attract a new customer than it is to keep an existing one."**

It is generally agreed that the next twelve months are going to be more competitive than the last twelve and there is an ever-growing focus on increasing profits. It is my sincere wish that companies begin to place more emphasis on pleasing their customers, and I hope that Tehrani's Law of Customer Service helps quantify why we all need to provide our customers with the best customer service in the 21$^{st}$ century."

**The historical view was that a bad customer experience results in someone telling 10 other people.**

*That could be harmful to a business but is usually not devastating. In the Age of the Internet however, the old rules are no longer valid. Online customer feedback is significantly amplified, giving anyone a megaphone to rave or rant about your Customer Care™ or lack thereof.*

In the nearly 15 years since first making my predictions, Customer Care™ has generally not improved. There are some unique examples of exceptional service commitment, but the reality is that very few organizations have cracked the code on consistent, engaging customer experiences.

That is why I am so pleased my company, Technology Marketing Corp. (TMC), is promoting this book. www.tmcnet.com

***Taking Your Customer Care™ to the Next Level*** **is needed now more than ever.**

If you apply the principles presented here and, "Go the Extra Mile" for the benefit of your customers, you will achieve extraordinary results and be able to lead in your field against even the mightiest of competitors.

## Even the Biggest of Brands Can Drop the Ball

It only takes one problem employee to create a public relations nightmare for a well-known and respected organization. DHL, FedEx, UPS and USPS are familiar with the concept of an employee dropping the ball, or quite literally a *package*.

The website www.dontthrowmypackage.com was "born in an effort to showcase, reveal and rectify the modern-day mishandling of human-delivered packages. Each year, worldwide, consumers and businesses alike spend billions of dollars on shipping and insurance services with the promise that their parcels will be handled with the care and service outlined in the selected dispatcher's rules and regulations. Quite frequently, as demonstrated on this website, employee performance doesn't always honor this promise — resulting in loss of time, money and goods and services."

"As the price of surveillance resources continues to drop, jilted package recipients have reluctantly turned to cameras and cellphones to capture neglectful, mishandled deliveries. With the advent of modern technology, 'It wasn't packed properly' no longer stands as the default line as damage and insurance claims are filed each year."

"Disheartened consumers and parcel recipients are entitled to the service they paid for and expect to receive. It is the mission of this website to offer resources and recourse to this group of growing individuals."

## Customer Care™ in the .SUCKS World

Today, with the advent of new domains, such as .Sucks, brands are literally being extorted to pay to protect their namesakes.

Social media requires companies to develop a line of defense in protecting their brands by offering the highest level of Customer Care™. We call this, *Next Level Customer Care™*.

*Nadji Tehrani; Steve Brubaker*

<u>But, how do you do it?</u>

The authors have designed a process shared in the pages of this book that you can use effectively to prevent a negative issue from becoming larger than life on social media.

You've heard the old adage, "Keep your friends close and your enemies closer". Well today upset customers must be kept close and allowed to vent directly to you so you can resolve the issue immediately before they take it to the social media airwaves.

Richard Tehrani, CEO of TMC

# Introduction:

**Companies Live or Die from Repeat Business:
Customer Retention Depends Upon Customer Care™**

Companies spend thousands of dollars to find just one new customer, yet they don't dedicate sufficient resources toward keeping their current customers. This book provides you with the tools you need to help you keep your customers, even when your competitors offer them a lower price.

**No Business Can Afford to Lose Customers...There is No Better Way to Keep Customers than to *Take Your Customer Care*™ *to the Next Level*.**

**No Customer, No Company...**

Because companies live or die from repeat business, we felt it was paramount for us to write this book to help our valued readers in maintaining more than 95 percent of their current customers. Without this approach, companies will likely not survive in today's super competitive business environment.

The editorial team behind this book has gone to great lengths in researching academic and professional literature to capture the thoughts of successful business leaders and learned scholars. We seek to apply many of these established principles and have also drawn from our own diverse business experiences to identify the best and most reliable solutions to *Take Your Customer Care*™

to the Next Level. We believe the practical steps outlined in the following chapters will create an advantage for your business that will be insurmountable for your competitors to match.

Ironically, as we searched for relevant experiences of companies with extraordinary Customer Care™, we had great difficulty finding more than a handful that have truly put the complete package together for *Taking Their Customer Care™ to the Next Level*. Many business leaders profess publicly to truly care for customers but fall short on execution.

A successful program of Customer Care™ must be designed and rolled out with a long term mentality. It is exceedingly more challenging to sustain the momentum beyond the initial communication of the philosophy.

**Most of the existing publications in circulation deal with providing customer satisfaction. <u>*Unfortunately today satisfying customers is not enough*</u>. You must go beyond customer satisfaction to the next level and go the extra mile on your customer's behalf.**

| **<u>Customer Satisfaction</u>** | **<u>Customer Care</u>**™ |
|---|---|
| Expectations are met | Expectations are exceeded |

Our hope is to help all readers enhance their Customer Care™ techniques to not only care for existing customers, but also generate new customers.

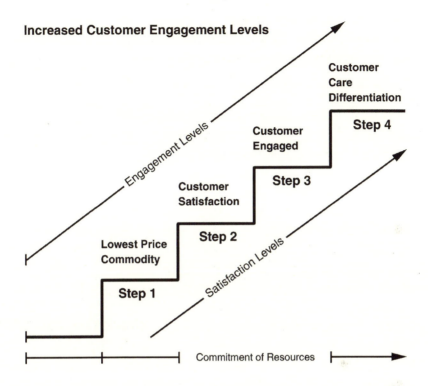

Providing increased levels of engagement is the single most important differentiator for companies today.

**Allow For Customized Experiences**

Remember Burger King's famous approach to, "Have it Your Way." The company seems to have abandoned the philosophy along with so many other organizations now delivering a cookie cutter approach to customer service. People are screaming to be appreciated as individuals. Embrace their needs and show you truly care. The result will be delighted customers who will become loyal advocates for your business.

**I CARE: The Core Philosophy**

"I CARE"...What refreshing words to hear in this world of automated marketing technology and self-service options. Not only is it comforting but it speaks directly to my desire for someone to really care about me as an individual consumer. I am not just a number in a queue or long line of customers waiting for assistance, <u>I am THE CUSTOMER, the ONLY CUSTOMER that matters in my own mind at the time, and I expect the very best service in the world.</u>

Employees of businesses today should give the same focus to each individual customer as they give to their favorite sports team during the championship game.

**As business owners and executives, we must lead by example to put the customers' needs at the forefront of our attention spans and develop our training, incentives, and policies to match the needs of the customer.**

Being attentive, efficient, engaging and friendly with those who are the lifeblood of our organization is not a marketing tactic; rather, it represents the core beliefs of the Customer Care™ philosophy.

Companies used to treat customers like they were the most important person on the planet and cater to their needs – the way our grandmothers must have been treated in the local full service department store. When she visited once each week she was immediately recognized by lifelong loyal employees who welcomed her as part of the store family. She would buy whatever she needed, and probably many things she didn't actually need. She was loyal to that store, rarely setting foot in the competing store across the street.

**Why? Because the workers there knew her, and cared for her needs. Indeed, they were her friends!**

Most everyone will agree with one of the most basic principles of business...that it is far more expensive to attract a new customer than it is to keep an existing customer. So then why do we not make existing customers our priority in everything we do, not just what we say?

For example, existing customers are often miffed when they notice retailers offering new customers a more attractive promotion that is not available to long-term, loyal customers.

**Is your advertising budget line item greater for customer acquisition as opposed to customer retention?**

If so, then you are losing the battle already. <u>Put more resources into your existing customers and they will stay loyal to you and become advocates for your company, your products, and your great service.</u> They will be your ambassadors to their families, friends and others in their everyday communications and to the world through social media.

19th century businessman, John Wanamaker opened the very first department store in the city of Philadelphia and is considered a marketing pioneer. The company thrived on innovation, offering a guaranteed cash refund to any customer who was not completely satisfied. Wanamaker is best known for the popular quote, "Half the money I spend on advertising is wasted; the trouble is I don't know which half." If he were alive today, he may be inclined to update the quote and say, along with many other frustrated corporate executives, "Half the money I spend on advertising is wasted, as I seem to be losing customers as quickly as I bring new ones in."

**Customer Care™ is about More Than Making a Sale, It Is about Building a Relationship**

To maintain your reputation, don't overpromise and under deliver... Rather, do the exact opposite: OVERDELIVER! Sales goals are short term tactics; relationship building is a long-term strategy.

<u>Most marketing and sales teams are incented to bring on new business. Their attention is NOT on Retention.</u>

Joe Porfeli, Founder of EIS and a telecommunications industry pioneer, established a clear customer retention philosophy for his sales team members. They were required to retain, at a minimum, 90% of their existing customers in order to receive full commission from their sales to new customers.

## How Important Are Customer Experiences?

Companies that invest in the customer experience will maintain a competitive edge. Still not convinced? Let's take a look at the numbers:

- *78 percent of consumers have left a transaction or not made an intended purchase because of a poor service experience, according to American Express.*
- *It costs up to 10 times more to acquire a new customer than it does to keep a current one, according to the White House Office of Consumer Affairs.*
- *3 in 5 customers would try a new brand or company for a better service experience, according to American Express.*
- *91 percent of unhappy customers will not willingly do business again with a company if they've received bad customer service, according to Lee Resources.*

Now that you are paying attention, take a look at the bottom line impact from *Taking Your Customer Care™ to the Next Level:*

- *The probability of selling to a new prospect is 5–20 percent, while the probability of selling to an existing customer is 60–70 percent, according to Marketing Metrics.*
- *On average, loyal customers are worth up to 10 times as much as their first purchase, according to the White House Office of Consumer Affairs.*
- *Resolving a complaint in the customer's favor means that customer will do business with you again 70 percent of the time, according to Lee Resources.*

## Customer Care™ Tactics and Channels

The specific approaches to caring for customers will vary based on the medium in which the communication with the customers takes place.

There are a growing number of channels today in which customers choose to relate to a business.

- Face to Face
- Phone Call
- Website
- Mobile and wearable technologies
- Text
- Social Media

Providing seamless continuity across all these platforms is essential to delivering world class Customer Care™. InContact conducted a research study through Harris Poll of U.S. adults online and found that today's consumers expect a number of channels to be readily accessible to them. In the order of importance to them are:

- Email (93 percent)
- 1-800 to Live Agent (81 percent)
- Online chat (67 percent)
- Mobile Apps (50 percent)
- SMS/Text message (46 percent)
- Social networking sites (39 percent)
- Online video chat (32 percent)

"Consumers expect a personalized, omni-channel customer journey that includes agent service continuity and choice of channels for follow-up communications," inContact said in a statement about the results. "A major goal of the study was to gauge consumer desire for personalized and omni-channel experiences when interacting with company representatives."

## B2C vs. B2B

Dealing with customers who are in businesses themselves requires a clear focus and caring philosophy. There are many nuances to what is called the business-to-business relationship. This book is applicable to all customer situations but is primarily designed to focus on the direct interface with end user customers, their experience with the company directly, and the care they must receive to be truly engaged. We will refer to this relationship as business to consumer, or B2C.

## Show Customers You Know the Difference between Right and Wrong

Some business leaders today define ethics as relative vs. absolute. Ethics involves doing what is right and is generally used to refer to how people should behave in a professional capacity.

Absolute ethics has traditionally been based on Judeo Christian values. It has only two sides: Something is good or bad, black or white. Clear examples of unethical behaviors are bribery, extortion, and perjury, which nearly everyone would agree are unacceptable.

Relative ethics implies the end justifies the means and is more complicated. It can have a multitude of sides with varying shades of gray. What is considered ethical behavior by one person may be deemed highly unethical by someone else.

USA Today cover stories abound based on lapses in the judgement of corporate leaders, that includes tales of:

- Separating tire treads
- Selling the "positive effects" of smoking
- Drug recalls
- Passengers trapped on the runway
- Faulty ignitions apparent in early testing
- Data breaches not disclosed immediately

We've all heard the stories. So what should you do?

**Do the Right Thing for the Right Reasons for Your Customers and You Will Be Rewarded with Their Trust, Loyalty and Respect.**

At the very heart of consumer trust there is both vulnerability and risk. There is a possibility of being exploited as compared to the benefit of continuing to pursue a relationship with an organization. Every customer makes an individual calculation, often subconsciously, prior to making a purchase or a re-purchase. As such, trust is the lens through which they view their experience with us.

**Don't Allow Your Business to be COMMODITIZED!**

If you are simply meeting customers' expectations today, your business will be perceived as a commodity and you will lose to your competition and ultimately become extinct. We have had great difficulty even finding true to life examples of genuine *Next Level Customer Care*™ in the many experiences we have personally encountered.

Now is the time to make a change and raise the bar of your customer experience process to new heights.

**Cut Customer Care™…Become a Commodity…Lose Competitive Advantage**

Companies live or die from repeat business! It bears repeating.

Some of you will read this, apply it and succeed. Others will wait and miss the opportunity and you will be on the outside looking in…We CAN HELP YOU…

*Nadji Tehrani; Steve Brubaker*

Visit us at:   http://www.nextlevelcustomercare.com

E-Mail:   customercarebook@tmcnet.com

Facebook:   Customer Care

Twitter:   @custcarebook

YouTube:   CustomerCare

**WE WILL HELP YOU** *Take Your Customer Care*™ *to the Next Level.*

## Chapter One

# CUSTOMER SATISFACTION IS NOT ENOUGH: YOU MUST GO THE EXTRA MILE

You may ask, "Is customer satisfaction enough?" Absolutely NOT today in a highly competitive environment! Customers are redefining for companies the way they expect to be cared for, which has resulted in a new paradigm. The structure and nature of that paradigm requires great leaders to keep their pulse on the environment and adapt to customers' evolving preferences. For example, are you relating to both the tech-savvy as well as the tech-averse consumer? Those who are less proficient in automated processes will require enhanced assistance to navigate technologically advanced products and services.

**The NEW Customer Care™ Relationship Paradigm**

Your website says...We put customers first, but you have a hold message when customers call that says, "we will answer your call in the order it was received." You have a line in your store for service with a sign that says to, "take a number."

**Take a Number...Seriously?**

If I am important to you as a business, then why don't you make me feel important when I reach out to you beyond just my initial purchase? Now we are not naive, we understand there are costs involved in staffing and that it is not possible to have immediate service for every customer at every moment of the day. (Dare we dream?)

Collectively with more than 60 years in the Customer Care™ industry, and experiencing the needs of thousands of clients firsthand, we understand that the desire is to provide the best service at the lowest cost. But companies MUST do better – the ones that DO will win their customers' hearts and wallets. Doing better does not mean telling the customer how important they are in a recording every few seconds as they hold for what seems like an eternity, waiting for assistance.

The New Customer Care™ Relationship Paradigm distinguishes those companies who create an experience that is second to none.

**New Customer Care Relationship Paradigm**

Customer expectations have been escalated by organizations like Amazon and Zappos, which are pushing through the upper boundary limits of Customer Care™ experience through the use of their specialized customer relationship management (CRM) technology. Their CRM systems do not only store my basic personal and financial information but utilize analytical and predictive capabilities to compare and contrast those products which are most likely to be of interest to me based on my past history. My search and purchase habits are correlated with those of customers of similar profiles to personalize my online experiences, and their recommendations are becoming surprising relevant. We refer to Next Level CRM as CEM: Customer Experience Management.

*Next Level Customer Care™* is no longer reserved for the elite. Whether your company is perceived as a luxury brand or a fledgling organization, consumers are demanding a "luxury experience" from you. Whether your customers pay a premium price for your services or not, they crave a superior level of customer service. Someday someone will likely find a way to undercut your price and unless your customer is so enamored with you due to the amazing care and service you provide, your business will be at risk.

**Proactive vs. Reactive Service Philosophy**

Savvy consumers now expect companies to be much more proactive to their needs rather than acting in a simply reactive manner. A recent study by inContact, found that 87 percent of customers want to be contacted proactively by companies with which they have existing relationships. Matt Marshall of VentureBeat states, "Certain sectors are more likely to be seen stepping up to the mark than others. Notable examples include banks and credit card companies now getting in touch by text and phone if they suspect fraudulent activity on your account. That could be potentially invaluable. Many online stores now prompt you about items that may be of interest to you, often long before you had even thought of getting the items. They must know us better than we know ourselves, as it is estimated that as many as 35 percent of Amazon sales are generated this way."

## The Customer Bill of Rights

Vanguard Communications, a consulting company in Rhode Island, has developed "The Customer Bill of Rights" consisting of the six inalienable rights that must be bestowed on each and every customer.

1. Know Me
2. Value Me as a Customer
3. Understand My Needs
4. Treat Me with Respect
5. Value My Time
6. Make it Easy

*Taking Your Customer Care™ to the Next Level* examines the real world view of issues today and provides specific and tangible tools for you to set your company apart from your competitors.

What if when your customers called, you knew who they were through your customer engagement technology platform and your front line employees greeted them by name, not asking them for their name, address, account number, etc.?

Being asked to provide personal information multiple times by multiple individuals in an organization is not a satisfactory customer experience. With transaction based cloud services being more effective and the costs continuing to drop, organizations of every size can use data analytics to capture basic information about the person calling even before your agent says, "Hello."

Now before we present the solutions, let's make sure we all understand clearly the problems in the primary service industry today. The bottom line is that consumers are generally not being delighted by companies today, with some rare exceptions. We share actual case studies and examples of experiences that were excellent and also those that should be shocking, if it weren't for the fact that poor customer experience has unfortunately become the norm in our society today. We will examine the airline industry in particular.

Customers expect the ability to interact across multiple channels (Internet, mobile, phone, catalog, retail) and choose to do business more often with companies that make the experience seamless when moving from one medium to another. Mobile connections are preferred most by today's generation age 25 and under. While the choice for online service experiences is growing, overall the phone remains the first channel customers choose when they want service. Expectations for excellent service are greatly reduced today as companies have been playing limbo with the Customer Care™ experience, seeing how low the bar may be lowered. True *Next Level Experiences* for customers will be immediately recognized and shared.

*Taking Your Customer Care™ to the Next Level* dispels the myths of cost containment where companies hope to find the cheapest service solution on the planet by sending "valued" customers around the globe where their experience is relegated to offshore outsourced call centers filled with people who have no first-hand knowledge of the needs of the American consumer and struggle to even speak the language clearly.

The bar is so low today that you can create a clear advantage for your company by being ready, able and willing to engage your own customers, AND those of your competitors. Learn how to use your service excellence as a "lethal weapon" against your industry counterparts. Uncover how to beat even the biggest of your industry foes by helping your customers experience what will seem like Nirvana when interacting with your business as opposed to what they are accustomed to when it comes to customer service.

In the following chapters, we will provide a step-by-step guide in developing the people and processes necessary to deliver excellent service that is consistent and repeatable. By advancing through increased levels of engagement based on delightful human interactions, your customers will become ambassadors with you, selling the benefits of your brand across their sphere of influence.

**Intelligent Customer Care™**

Your service approach must be flexible to be in-sync with the emotional needs of your customers. Not every person reaching out to do business with you is looking for a "warm and fuzzy" experience. "Fast and efficient" or "convenient and timely" are equally important to many customers.

Have you ever headed to the local grocery store late at night when it was raining and you threw on an old sweatshirt and jeans? Going through the service line to pay for your milk and cookies, you may not be trying to connect with the employee as a soulmate. You just want to make the purchase quickly and efficiently and get back home to the final episode of "Downton Abbey" on Netflix. You are not looking to spend time in conversation.

Adapting to the unique clues and signals customers provide and personalizing our Customer Care™ to fit the situation at that specific point in time will be recognized and appreciated.

**Nurture Your Customers**

Do your customers recognize the care you provide and evangelize on behalf of your brand? Are new customers reaching out to you and letting you know they heard about your great service from a friend, colleague or family member? Great customer experiences will never be hid under a bushel – they will be SHARED! People love to tell a good story, so let's give them something to talk about by providing *Next Level Customer Care*™ to those who choose to do business with us!

## Be Sincere

Never doubt the impact of sincerity in Customer Care™. Face to face interactions are a great way to engage with individual customers. Look your customer in the eyes, smile and express true empathy. Show your customers you are more than a voice in the receiver or an automated online attendant. Deliver a real life human one-to-one interaction showing you care about the issue at hand on a personal level.

Let's face it. Your brand is defined by the interactions customers have with you, and not by the promotional messages you pay so dearly to advertise. Actual customer experiences will ultimately dictate whether an individual will trust your message and choose to continue interacting with your brand.

## Satisfaction is Just the Start

David Krajicek Ph.D., CEO GfK Consumer Experiences North America states, "Loyalty is not the same as affinity. Brand loyalty may be just a series of transactions: A consumer buys the same product for a period of months, so he must be loyal."

He suggests companies once believed that quality alone was the key to loyalty and success. "But with competition so intense, quality, while still important to satisfaction, is not enough to assure a brand is chosen. Brand experiences need to be not just satisfactory but memorable. This is the difference between building simple loyalty, by meeting traditional, one-dimensional goals, and creating affinity, something more personal and indelible."

David goes on to express the critical need for measuring the right data and being flexible with choosing your metrics. He believes, "Consumer information is the engine of customer satisfaction.

To do more and better is not just possible but essential because the competition has the same resources and perhaps the same commitment to focus. To the brand with the strongest grasp on consumer relationships will go the spoils of deep satisfaction and loyalty."

Companies like Apple, Nike and Starbucks connect emotionally with their consumers who are intensely loyal to the brand. These companies have developed immunity against the competitive attacks from low priced alternatives.

**Go the Extra Mile**

Meeting expectations is not going to win the hearts and minds of your customers.

You must, *"Go the Extra Mile"* and exceed customer expectations.

The co-authors of this book, Nadji Tehrani and Steve Brubaker initially met at TMC's first Customer Care™ trade show, TBT 1986, in Atlanta. Nadji is considered the founder of the industry and Steve was eager to learn from him and gain industry insight that played a significant role in developing his career. In the decades since, Nadji and Steve have continued to work together and as a result have become good friends.

 Nadji Tehrani offers here an example of how one business he encountered went the extra mile:

""I was visiting friends in the Midwest and tripped on a loose brick in the pavement outside their office one afternoon, hitting the corner of my eyebrow on a rock. I was shaken a bit, but was OK; however, the gash near my eye was bleeding. My friends took me to a nearby medical facility. The doctor there carefully examined me and identified no bones were broken; I just had a few bruises. She cleaned the area around my eye with the cut, and put six stitches in place. She was very kind and we spoke of our families in some detail while she was completing her work. I left feeling exceptionally well and thanked her and my friends profusely for taking such outstanding care of me while I was away from home."

"I needed to travel home by plane later that evening to return to my media and publishing company, TMC, where we publish the print and digital <u>CUSTOMER</u> and <u>INTERNET TELEPHONY</u> magazines, as well as host industry leading conferences, online news and information at www.tmcnet.com."

Caring Beyond the Business Transaction

"As I was working in the office the following day, a call came in from the doctor who had cared for me just the day before. She asked how I was feeling and if I had experienced any difficulty on the return trip home. We talked for a while, and it was as if she was a member of my own family in the way she showed genuine concern for me."

"I don't know about you, but I was taken back by this call from the doctor. That is certainly not the level of Customer Care™ I was accustomed to experiencing. This doctor epitomizes what it takes today to go the extra mile and make a lasting impression with your customers – caring beyond the business transaction. I could tell in her voice and mannerisms when I was in her office that she really did care. This call the next day cemented that fact in my mind. If I were to ever move to the Midwest state where my friends live, I assure you she would be first on my list for medical care for me and my family."

**"The bottom line is…If you want to *Take Your Customer Care*™ *to the Next Level* you must be willing to *Go the Extra Mile*… AND, there is No Shortcut.""**

Chapter Two

# TAKING CARE OF YOUR CUSTOMERS TAKES CARE OF YOUR BUSINESS

No one likes the word, <u>Complaint</u>. The term <u>Opportunity</u> is preferred instead when referring to customer concerns. Whenever a customer confronts you with an issue, try not to view this in a negative way, but see it as an opportunity to engage with the individual and determine what will make the customer appreciate your Customer Care™ efforts.

**"I <u>WILL</u> Help You!"**

The words, "I will help you" are quite effective, almost magical, when approached by a customer who clearly needs resolution. This works far better than asking, "How may I help you?" You see, people are so used to experiencing poor service and an uncaring response when sharing their problems with a business owner or employee that they EXPECT to not really be heard. When asked, "How may I help you?" the first reaction is often to ratchet up the emotional level of their plea to gain some leverage in what they believe will be a complex negotiation. The word, "May" gives the impression they *May or May Not* get help, and they expect they won't.

When you make it clear up front that customers WILL be helped and then listen carefully to them, they are immediately put at ease. That is not the accustomed response. They have to think for a moment before continuing. Then they are more relaxed and can explain why they need assistance.

Of course, you DO actually have to deliver on your promise. By saying the words, "I Will Help You," I am immediately put in a position to be that customer's advocate and take responsibility for making him or her happy.

## Avoid Confrontation, Promote Resolution

The resolution does not have to be exactly what customers state they want done.

We cannot put the business in a financial hardship or give away the store. Customers know this and are rarely unreasonable especially when they know you really do care about them and desire their complete satisfaction and loyalty.

There will be challenging customers. They will be 100 percent RIGHT in their own mind. Accept it and move on.

## **Remember...The Customer Is Always Right!**

## Listening

Are employees really listening to the customer? Are they providing uninterrupted eye contact in a face-to-face encounter? Is their body language welcoming, inviting and non-confrontational?

Or in a phone conversation, are they giving positive signs of reinforcement as they are listening intently – saying things such as, "Yes, Oh my, I see," or other genuine acknowledgement to individuals as they share their feelings?

Here are a few rules to remember for better listening skills:

- Do not to interrupt someone when they are talking. After all, we should listen to people the way we want them to listen to us when it is our turn to speak.
- When possible, go to a quiet place with few distractions. Listening becomes easier when you only have to listen to one voice at a time.
- Quiet your own thoughts if something is bothering you. You are less likely to listen to what the other person is saying if you are focused more on listening to your own thoughts.
- Actions speak louder than words. Your body language shows how ready or open you are to listening.
- When asked for a response, a simple nod of agreement or an "uh-huh" may suffice. Open-ended questions work well, such as, "How did you feel about that?" or, "What happened next?"
- Shut up! Especially if the other person is emotional. Grab a box of tissue and a glass of water as appropriate. Be a compassionate listener. The ability to shut up at the right moment will make a difference in their perception of you as a good listener.

## Use the 3 F's to diffuse the situation

- Feel: I recognize how you Feel...
- Felt: I've Felt that way myself in similar circumstances...
- Found: But I have Found that we can resolve the issue by...

Then make the difference for their individual need and accommodation. Find something to meet their need and satisfy them by showing you CARE.

Take action based on what you've heard and learn from it proactively to prevent the same situation from happening again with future customers.

For example, customers often have to deal with small print and hard to read instructions on product labels. Taking action to deal with the problem could take the form of printing larger and simpler instructions on the packaging or providing a separate large print instruction sheet.

**Empathize: No One Cares What You Know Until They Know That You Care**

It may sound sentimental at first, but an important variable in *Next Level Customer Care*™ is Empathy. Think about a recent positive interaction you've experienced with a company; the employee(s) probably conveyed genuine engagement and concern regarding your service inquiry—that is, he or she was empathetic toward your situation.

According to NewVoiceMedia, poor customer relations cost companies nearly $41 billion each year. But this doesn't have to be the case. Preserve relationships by providing the utmost compassion for your customers.

When empathy is missing from a company's mission, unfavorable scenarios ensue. For example, an unpleasant American Airlines Customer Care™ blunder involved a woman spending six hours on hold. It's clear the Customer Care™ representative lacked empathy for the woman's needs as she was neglected for several hours. As a result, American Airlines' reputation suffered; for instance, the company has received a multitude of unfavorable comments on its Twitter page.

But expressing empathy means more than a prompt response. Rather, this characteristic should touch all of your business's Customer Care™ best practices, down to dealing with instances of bad reviews. For example, one hotel went so far as to fine its customers $500 for posting negative reviews on Yelp. Rather than fight fire with fire or try to cover up negative press, businesses should use poor reviews as a learning experience and motivation to improve their Customer Care™ strategy. Businesses that receive unfavorable assessments can redeem their reputation by expressing compassion for customers' unpleasant experiences. For example, turn around a bad experience by offering up an honest apology and making a commitment toward improving future services.

How can you ensure your team members are prepared to provide the highest level of empathy? Here a few ways:

- Routinely observe employee interactions with customers more frequently to maintain consistent quality.
- Provide employees with positive reinforcement for above and beyond quality of Customer Care™.
- Use technology to identify customer preferences and act on the knowledge to create more personalized experiences.
- Hire the right staff, i.e., make sure your potential candidates exhibit maturity, experience and dedication to their work.

The bottom line is this: Never underestimate the power of empathy; it might be the most powerful tool in customer retention.

**Don't Repeat Angry Words**

When customers are irritated and express their anger, listen intently and respond with caring words, but don't repeat their negative words.

Some employees misunderstand that when we say, 'Empathize with the Customer', they are to repeat the situation back exactly as the customer presented it so the person will recognize they have been heard. Restating harsh and negative words will often have the same effect as adding fuel to a fire. A calm demeanor and soothing words are much more effective to help de-escalate an issue.

## Apologize: "I AM Sorry…"

Companies are beginning to invest a lot of time and effort in figuring out what customers want and need, and delivering solutions and support to meet those requirements and even exceed expectations. But sometimes the solution to a customer support problem is as plain as the nose on your face. And that solution is to speak two simple words: I'm sorry.

This advice comes courtesy of Scott Broetzmann, founder of Customer Care Measurement and Consulting, which with Arizona State University conducts and publishes studies on customer rage. They have found that oftentimes the things that people want don't cost anything. Rather, what many customers who report a less than delightful experience are seeking is what Broetzmann refers to as psychological currency, which basically, is an apology.

Owning up to the situation and saying you are sorry shows you are ready to take responsibility. Then move forward with what went wrong and what you are doing to ensure the situation has been completely handled and will not reoccur. If you don't explain, people will wonder if you are paying attention and make their own assumptions. Make sure you have done research into the issue and are prepared with the facts. It is best to respond with the appropriate answers instead of just rushing out with a general apology that may seem insincere without specifics. Also, make sure that your corrective action is implemented without fail. You only get one bite of the apology apple. Saying, "I'm Sorry" is a good policy, provided you are sincere, and express taking responsibility.

## Don't Allow, "I'm Sorry" To Be an Excuse but Rather an Action to Own the Issue and Correct It

Customer's goals when complaining are to get their problems resolved, 44 percent though said they would be satisfied with a simple apology rather than a refund, according to Consumer

Action Monitor. Nip concerns in the bud, so they do not go any further – or worse, escalate to the media, a government entity or judge and jury.

Even when you feel the customer's story borders on hyperbole, the only course of action that will make a difference is to take responsibility.

Consumer Action Monitor researched escalated complaints that were taken to a third party, and found:

- 58 percent were provided to a government watchdog, representing regulatory action risk for the company involved
- 27 percent were shared on social media
- 9 percent contacted a media agent to tell their story
- 6 percent took legal action, which could result in significant defense and/or settlement costs

The study also concluded that 50 percent of consumers think more highly of a business after their complaint is handled well.

Dealing with consumer opportunities is a key part of your company's reputation management, whether you are a large corporation or a small business. Even when you make some kind of business mistake, it is important to address the issue appropriately. Not knowing what to say is not an excuse to be silent.

**Don't Allow Others to Control Your Message**

You need to control your message. Publish a point of contact to allow for direct communication with your office, and prepare a team to talk with those who have questions or want to express personal concern. It is better for them to speak directly with you than to vent on social media or contact the press or government officials. Your prompt and trustworthy action will diffuse much of the grandstanding and will likely result in some public recognition by others for your candid efforts.

**No Excuses**

The soothing effects of you saying, "I am sorry" will be quickly negated if you make retaliatory attacks or use the apology to defend your position.

Former Food Network star, Paula Deen, was blasted for not showing remorse in 2013 during her infamous Today Show interview with Matt Lauer. Crisis expert David E. Johnson, CEO of the PR and branding firm Strategic Vision, told Entertainment Weekly that Deen sent the wrong message: "She acted like she was the wronged party," he said. "Paula is known as a woman who is a gregarious, nice grandma. Instead, she came across as angry and mean. She says she is the victim."

We all want to correct misinformation, but an apology should be an apology with no spin. All the good work you do can be reinforced in your go forward communications, but should not be part of your apology. After people believe your words and re-establish trust, they will be more open to listening to your advertisements.

**Become a Customer Chameleon**

Providing relatable Customer Care™ requires being adaptable, similar to a chameleon changing colors to blend with its environment. Listen carefully to the tone and mood of each customer, and use a similar individualized approach to develop rapport with the person. Customer Care™ must be flexible, and there is no one method or approach that works in every situation. Recognize that everyone you come into contact with possesses unique personality traits. By attempting to understand them and adapt to their personal circumstances, they will be more likely to respond positively to you.

## Goods vs. Services

There are differences in the ways customers gauge their experiences with the manufacturers of physical products as compared to companies providing services.

Collectively, services industries account for more than 70 percent of the U.S. GNP. Service organizations emphasize people, ideas and information instead of things. Most of us are familiar with companies that offer a blend of goods and services in their relationships with consumers.

A special dining experience is memorable because of the quality and presentation of the food, the attentiveness and courtesy of the server, as well as the atmosphere and comfort of the environment and furniture. When choosing to visit a fast service restaurant like Chipotle or Chick-fil-A, is it for good food or prompt service? It depends on the circumstances: Whether you're with or without children, seeking a quick lunch or a leisurely dinner.

The U.S. Census Bureau classifies services organizations into numerous categories, such as:

- Lodging
- Personal services
- Business services
- Repair services
- Recreation services
- Health services
- Legal services
- Educational services
- Social services
- Noncommercial institutions
- Membership organizations

Each of these service industries engage with the public in unique ways and must develop people and processes to not only meet the needs of customers but exceed their highest level of expectations and create delightful experiences to keep them coming back for more. And most service industries such as business services can be segmented further into areas such as marketing services, all the way down to specific channels, such as social media services.

## Customer Care™ Quality Counts

Dr. Leonard Berry, Distinguished Professor at Texas A&M University, developed a framework for managing service experience clues. He writes that, "Customers consciously and unconsciously filter experience clues and organize them into a set of impressions, some more rational or calculative and others more emotional."

He goes on to explain that if the customer can "see, hear, taste, or smell it, it is a clue." Researchers in marketing have studied in depth the effects of lighting, scent and music. The U.S. Small Business Administration promotes that music boosts employee productivity and morale. And selecting the right music will keep customers in a store longer.

According to Gallup Organization Studies, slow tempo music increased per dinner party bar sales 40.9 percent, restaurant diners lingered 24 percent longer when slow tempo music played, and 33 percent of shoppers cited that music played in a store influenced their decision to make a purchase.

Dr. Berry makes the case that exceeding customer service expectations requires exceeding their basic expectations, "An accurate bank statement and hot water in the hotel's shower do not evoke surprise. They do not make customers say, 'Wow, this is a great experience.'"

The esthetics of a business environment creates certain impressions for the customer experience. Barnes & Noble encourages customers to spend time in its bookstores. It offers comfortable chairs, large open areas, Starbucks coffee, and clean restrooms. Customers are invited to relax and browse.

Dr. Berry makes it clear though that the human clues created by employees are the most critical and lasting for establishing a bond with the customer. He states that, "Human interaction in the service experience offers the chance to cultivate emotional connectivity that can extend respect and esteem to customers and, in so doing, exceed their expectations, strengthen their trust, and deepen their loyalty."

## Quality of Service Rests with Your People

Service companies are highly dependent on individuals to perform the services. More than 80 percent of all newly created jobs are a result of growth in the service sector. Variability must be minimized to consistently deliver a quality interaction. The quality of the service experience is determined by customers based on their expectations. When expectations are met, the experience is perceived as satisfactory, but when expectations are exceeded, customers are delighted and rate the experience as exceptional.

Disney is a leader in planning for quality engagement in minute detail at every stage of the customer experience. Cast members welcome travel weary guests at their cars when they arrive and staff parking areas with roving rescue teams assisting visitors with car trouble. They also greet guests directly at the airport when approaching baggage claim to board Disney's Magical Express transportation whisking them directly to their resort hotel or cruise terminal.

## Customer Experience Disconnects

Identifying gaps when customer experiences do not match expectations is critical to developing a world class service organization. There are several main gap areas companies should be looking to identify and correct:

## Customer Wishes vs. Company Perceptions

If the customer is expecting more advanced services than your company plans to provide, there will be an immediate disconnect. For example, rental car agencies cannot simply provide fast and friendly counter service with a selection of clean reliable cars.

National Car Rental Emerald Club raises the bar by eliminating the wait for customers who choose any car waiting in the appropriate row, hop in and drive away. Waiting at the counter is no longer acceptable for travelers, regardless of a friendly service team.

We never wait for a car and are always able to choose a full-size model even though we reserve and pay for the standard midsize vehicle.

## Company Perceptions vs. Company Standards

Companies many times determine at the senior management level to provide a certain level of service, but do not put the necessary staff and other resources in place to deliver it.

Have you visited a business, such as a bank branch, at lunchtime during the standard workweek to request assistance and notice employees of that company walking out the door themselves for lunch? Clearly the appropriate design for a business is to hire team members to work the hours when customers are most likely to visit or call. Managers should be aware of the flow of customer traffic to the business and schedule to meet the demand.

**Management must Adapt, Be Flexible and Move Resources to Meet Demand**

 Steve Brubaker, one of the authors of this book, offers a personal experience on this front:

"I recently traveled to a major US tourist destination and made a reservation with one of the most highly regarded luxury brand hotels. Upon arriving I was impressed with the beautifully ornate surroundings. I entered the hotel lobby and immediately was surrounded with the engaging aroma of freshly cut roses and orchids. I was certain my experience would be memorable."

"Noticing the elite service desk was not staffed that Saturday afternoon, I approached the concierge desk and asked for assistance. There were two concierge employees with no other customers, yet I was instructed to join a registration line where a number of others waited to check-in. Not wanting to be overly impatient I went to the line which slowly moved along. Both cashiers were busy with individuals who needed in-depth attention, so while waiting I looked around for alternative sources of help. I noticed a valet desk also staffed with two employees, yet no customers. In addition, there were several management level staff members standing around, apparently oblivious to the growing line of arriving customers."

## "You Don't Need Four Managers to Oversee Two Workers"

"Those of us in line began to grumble as the line came to a complete stop for what seemed like an eternity. I motioned to one of the managers and asked if they could get some additional help to the front desk. He went to the back office and soon another manager emerged and joined the front desk team. However, instead of calling a customer to the desk, she stood there typing into a computer looking down and never making eye contact with those of us waiting in line."

"Finally, there was an opening for me to be served by one of the other clerks. She was very nice and apologized for the delay. She took my identification and shared that I should not have waited in line, but was eligible to go directly to the VIP Room for check-in. She escorted me to a private area where I was given my keys and other instructions by another helpful and very professional staff member."

- "Why didn't the concierge offer this VIP experience to me when I asked?"
- "Why weren't the idle staff members cross-trained to help customers as needed?"
- "And most importantly, why weren't the managers jumping in and caring for the customers?"

"The remainder of my stay was absolutely fantastic. The service offered by the restaurant, housekeeping and other staff was unmatched by any other hotel I have visited. My suite and amenities were second to none. Unfortunately for this company though, my first impression can never be replaced. The management clearly failed me and their hard-working employees by not creating a process to handle variations in customer demand, as well as by not facilitating clear communication among the various department teams.""

Company Standards vs. Employee Actions

If the company's employees deliver service below the company's standard it will be impossible to delight the customer.

We have all experienced a situation where an employee dropped the ball.

**Are you a WAITER or a SERVER?**

Steve:

""I've never liked the title, "waiter" in a restaurant. I don't like to wait to be helped and since the title implies a wait, forget it. When a server delights me with excellent care, I am happy. Either way I will tell others about the experience, good or bad."

"I visited a popular sandwich cafe to place an order for coffee late one afternoon. No other customers were at the counter, and two employees were available to provide assistance. One was talking to someone in the kitchen through the wall opening. The other was making notes at the register and didn't acknowledge me. After about 30 seconds, she finally looked up and said, 'I'll be with you in a moment.' I noticed a friend at a nearby table and turned to say, hello. Two other customers walked up at the other end of the counter, and the same waiter went over and took their order. I had to walk to the separate counter as well and wait in line behind these next customers to order after they were finished. Had either of the two available employees taken ownership as a server and helped me appropriately when I first approached the counter, I would be sharing a much better experience.'"

## Company Actions vs. Company Communications

There's a difference between promises in the company's advertisement or promotion and actual customer experience.

A common pricing strategy for retailers is to mark up their standard pricing so their promotion price is the price customers actually pay, and the price the company expected to receive all along. When consumers find the sale item at another retailer for the same price without discount, the pricing integrity comes into question. It will become almost impossible going forward for the original company to get customers back without continued promotion.

Macy's, Kohl's and JCPenney have all programmed customers to expect a sale each and every week of the year. If I don't have a coupon in hand, you can forget about me even going through their doors. Why would I ever pay their "regular" prices as they are clearly inflated due to their ongoing and aggressive promotional strategies?

The effects hit home for JCPenney a few years back when a new CEO removed all incentives and created an everyday low price approach. The company's customers evaporated, and the beautifully redesigned stores were devoid of activity. The CEO was dismissed, and the company returned to its former aggressive promotional strategy. It had created a perception in customers' minds that the value of the brand is in the discount, and there was no turning back.

Dillard's and Nordstrom have storewide sales only a few times per year which creates a feeling of being special and unique. It is rare to find the lower prices any other time of the year in those stores.

**Customer Care™ Package in SEVEN P's:**

Exceeding customer expectations requires carefully executing a well-designed service strategy. The Seven P's will help prepare your care package to deliver on your promises. Ensure you have:

1. The Right Product at...
2. The Right Point in Time in...
3. The Right Place at...
4. The Right Price with...
5. The Right Promotion...
6. Passing through the Right Channel Path with...
7. The Right Presentation

Variability in the personalities of employees can greatly impact customer experience. A doctor's bedside manner, courtesy of a grocery store clerk, or efficiency of a bank teller require ensuring the right people are in the right roles. Excellence in hiring, training, motivation and employee engagement will ensure you are able to retain loyal customers.

**Customer Care™ Communication**

Use the right language to communicate with your customers. Doing that clearly shows your commitment to caring for them and their needs. The right language is whichever language the customer prefers. Service providers need to adjust their language to fit the demographic profile of the customer. You do this by first listening in order to determine the appropriate response to the customer's needs.

Michael Hess of MoneyWatch recommends businesses use "six active, enthusiastic, mood-altering, wonderfully human words that will dramatically change the way customers react to your conversations, e-mails and text chats."

"Delighted"
"Absolutely"
"Pleasure"
"Happy"
"Sorry"
"Yes"

Hess writes, "Think of the passive catch-all, 'Let me see what I can do,' which sets the customer's expectations somewhere between low and zero. But change that to 'I'd be delighted to help' and the customer will be smiling, confident that you're actually interested in helping her."

Chick-fil-A's "my pleasure" policy instituted by the company's founder, S. Truett Cathy, was inspired by a visit to the Ritz-Carlton. When Cathy said "thank you" to the man behind the counter, he responded, "My pleasure." Out of this exchange, Chick-fil-A's novel idea was born: "Treat customers as if they're at a luxury establishment." The model continues to distinguish Chick-fil-A from its competitors, highlighting the importance of the little ways you communicate with customers.

## Perceived Value

Customer perceived value is price sensitive but luxury brands that deliver the highest quality service experiences are easily able to command a premium.

*Nadji Tehrani; Steve Brubaker*

**Putting on the Ritz**

Steve:

""I was traveling on a plane recently while doing some research for this book. I was reading another book about The Ritz-Carlton and its near obsession with customer personalization and engagement."

"Ken Boyd, managing partner of The Way Investment Advisors in Cleveland Ohio, was seated next to me. He introduced himself and asked why I was interested in The Ritz-Carlton. Ken was very nice, and so we talked about some of our past customer experiences, good and bad. He shared details of his visit to the Ritz-Carlton Montego Bay in Jamaica. I had also stayed at that particular hotel and was personally familiar with the breathtakingly beautiful facility and location."

"Ken shared that he and his wife were part of a group of investment advisors invited to Jamaica for a week by Merrill Lynch. When they arrived at the hotel, apparently the rooms had been overbooked and there were no available rooms for their party. The gracious Ritz-Carlton employees apologized and offered lunch and service at the pool for the afternoon while they worked to resolve the issue."

"Unfortunately by the end of the day, the hotel was unable to accommodate 7 of the couples with rooms. The Ritz-Carlton provided a bus and escorted the guests to another hotel nearby, although it was not nearly as nice as The Ritz-Carlton. Several staff members stayed with the guests at the other hotel, caring for their every need and whim that evening. The next morning the bus returned them to The Ritz-Carlton and all 7 couples were upgraded to magnificent suites for the remainder of the week."

"Ken told me that the disappointment of their first night was more than made up by the red carpet treatment they received for the rest of their stay. He explained that small details were noticed by the staff such as the unsweetened ice tea he ordered the first day was delivered each subsequent day for lunch almost immediately as he sat down. He never had to ask for it again."

"After returning, a few weeks later, a large package arrived at his home. It was meticulously wrapped and when opened, inside were two Ritz-Carlton plush robes, two Ritz-Carlton pillows, a $500 Ritz-Carlton gift certificate and a voucher for two free night's future stay at any Ritz-Carlton property in the world."

"Ken took his wife later that year to Paris and they stayed, guess where? That's right...The Ritz-Carlton! Ken continues to tell the story several years later, and it is always well received.""

**Never Cease Serving Your Customers**

An attitude of Customer Care™ overcomes the feeling that, "they are just trying to sell me something." If I project to customers that I am more concerned for their needs, and do anything and everything possible to help them, they are more likely to place their trust in me and in return give me their business.

Steve:

""My father in law, Hal Foster, recently retired from his successful financial services practice. He shared a story of one large business owner he worked with, who needed help with his personal retirement planning. Hal met with the man numerous times to carefully understand his needs and delivered a unique solution tailored to his situation. The man was so pleased he asked his company CFO to call Hal the next week. The company hired him as its exclusive financial consultant. He also developed pension plans for all the corporation executives."

"By having a service philosophy first, the customer will place more trust in you and develop a willingness to offer you increased levels of loyalty.""

## Exceptional Customer Care™ is a Game Changer

Your personal approach to caring for your customers is likely unique to your business and the basis for the special experience you provide your audience. Here are some "do's" and "don'ts" for implementing a *Next Level Customer Care™* program:

Don't Go It Alone

Some business owners and managers want to personally handle their customer relationships. They get involved with every customer issue and have difficulty entrusting their team with responsibility.

Enable Technology

Many of the routine tasks you and your staff perform can be streamlined. Operational efficiency must be part of your strategic plan in creating ideal customer experiences.

Disney's MyMagic+ initiative is a billion dollar investment that is a combination of a website, a mobile application and a wristband that collectively allow visitors to customize their experiences at a Disney park.

KISS - Keep it Simple and *SMART*

You ARE Smart. Sometimes though, we all over-analyze things. If you are asking your team to track minutia, they will do exactly as you train them. But don't be surprised if the customer experience becomes laborious and lacks spontaneity. Your process should focus on metrics that are essential: *Track the things that really matter!* Determine what information you will need to use in making your service better for the customer.

## Bleeding Edge

Some companies want to impress customers with technology. If it makes sense and works to improve the customer experience, then by all means, use technology to your advantage. Don't add technology for the sake of technology. Also, don't assume that technology alone will make customers more interested in doing business with you. People do business with people and appreciate personal connection.

Steve:

""I visited a repair shop to replace the cracked screen on my wife's iPad. When I arrived, there was no one to greet me, only a computer with a sign that instructed me to enter my name and some personal information first. Then someone would be 'with me.'"

"I was not about to provide personal details until I talked with a knowledgeable person, found out the cost and timing of service, and decided whether or not to do business with the shop.""

## Be Reasonable

When customers ask for a favor, try to grant their request. Don't rely on the proverbial, "that is not our policy." Sure, policies are designed to protect the business, but the best way to ensure your business success is to make customers happy – to do favors and make people feel special. Your employees are happier too when they don't have to tell customers, no for no good reason.

Steve:

"When I go to a store that is advertising a promotion but I forget to bring the coupon they sent to me at home, I expect them to still honor the discount on the spot. When they do, I am pleased and keep them at the top of my list for a return visit."

All complaint areas should result in a root cause analysis from the review of case study examples to correct systemic issues. Complaints tell us where the process is painful for the customer and where the experience creates dissatisfaction.

The rule of thumb is that only one in 10 customers will even tell you when they are unhappy. Perhaps the message from their mother still sticks for some people. "If you don't have anything nice to say, don't say anything at all." In today's social world, this group is dwindling as negative online rants are quite common. Companies need their customers to bring complaints directly to the source. Why is this not happening more than 10 percent of the time? Consider the following issues:

Lack of Confidence in Getting Resolution

Why should customers bother complaining if they have little hope anything will be done? Service providers need to be transparent and helpful in their dealings with customers to show they are listening and desire open communication.

Complaining is a Hassle

The expected time involved in even finding someone to actually listen to a concern creates a barrier. Speed and efficiency in your communication channels will prove you are prepared and ready to hear from your valuable customers.

Fear of Retaliation

Some personalities naturally avoid any type of confrontation. They will be more likely to tell friends and family but wouldn't engage directly in an uncomfortable discussion. These people speak with their feet before risking retaliation.

**Steve:**

"″I have had friends tell me they never complain at a restaurant, as they are afraid of what might happen to their food behind closed doors."

"Encourage open and honest criticism from your customers. Use their feedback to take corrective action and change what is causing the concern, which could easily result in up to ten times more delighted customers.″"

## Immediacy MUST be Core to your Customer Care™ Culture

Immediacy needs to be considered carefully by companies today. Mobile and online applications have elevated customers' expectations for companies to provide service that is timely and dynamic, location-sensitive, and reflective of their wants and needs. Overnight delivery is today's reality.

## Are Malls Missing the Mark?

It is no secret that the sprawling suburban mall store environment is suffering from customer neglect. Today, people are drawn to freshly developed lifestyle centers with entertainment, dining and shopping venues all interconnected. Many of these new retail environments resemble the thriving downtowns of yesteryear, including townhouse and apartment living options. Big box and specialty retailers are aware and trying to keep up with the modern consumer's evolving expectations. When someone can drive right to your door, park and enter your store, there is convenience and security.

## What is Your Brand Promise?

A strong brand promise is one that connects your purpose, your positioning, your strategy, your people and your customer experience. It enables you to deliver your brand in a way that connects emotionally with your customers and differentiates your company.

Here are a few examples of companies that have defined their brands in a way in which we easily connect and remember:

- BMW: "The Ultimate Driving Machine"
- Geico: "15 minutes or less can save you 15% or more on car insurance."
- Harley Davidson: "We are Harley Davidson."
- Walmart: "Save money. Live better."

**Ace Hardware Delivers**

In February 2015 Ace Hardware, the largest retailer-owned hardware cooperative, announced the rollout of its latest pilot program designed to further extend Ace's helpful brand promise as the company continues to add new ways to serve the needs of customers and attract new shoppers. Ace's Express Delivery program allows customers to find the products they need on acehardware.com and have them delivered by a helpful associate from their neighborhood Ace the same day.

"With 4,400 stores stocking the most locally relevant product assortments, Ace has a unique opportunity to become a big player in the same day delivery landscape once our pilot program concludes," said John Surane, executive vice president of marketing, merchandising, and sales at Ace Hardware Corp. "About 61 percent of consumers across the country live within five miles of their neighborhood Ace, and that proximity to the household sets us apart. The Ace Hardware brand has always been synonymous with helpful and excellent customer service, so Express Delivery from your local Ace store represents a perfect extension of our brand promise -- Amazing Every Customer, Every Time."

Taking care of your business today requires defining a clear set of guiding principles that must be communicated and understood throughout the organization. Emphasize the EXPERIENCE you will provide to each and every customer as your brand promise.

Over-deliver on your promises to *Take Your Customer Care*™ *to the Next Level.*

Chapter Three

# MARKETING DEFINED IN THE AGE OF AUTOMATION

Businesses that use marketing automation to nurture prospects experience a 451 percent increase in qualified leads, according to The Annuitas Group.

Marketing automation drives a 14.5 percent increase in sales productivity and a 12.2 percent reduction in marketing overhead, according to Nucleus Research.

By 2020, customers will manage 85 percent of their relationships without talking to a human, according to Gartner Research.

**Marketing automation** refers to software platforms and technologies designed for **marketing** departments and organizations to more effectively market on multiple channels online (such as email, social media, websites, etc.) and **automate** repetitive tasks.

The goal of marketing is to increase awareness for products and services and thereby create qualified leads, which historically required significant creative resource efforts. Automation results in making things happen with as little human intervention as possible.

The shift to online media opened the door for automation to trickle into the world of marketing. In the digital world, marketers can see not only what messaging works but who responds and how those people have interacted with the brand in the past. By bringing all that data together and mapping the various consumer paths, marketers can automatically personalize content to prospects and customers.

Paula Bernier, executive editor at TMC, explains: "The always-on consumer, artificial intelligence, automation, big data, cloud communications, digitization, mobility, and good old-fashioned competition are transforming marketing as we know it. People and companies that had once used a combination of art and experience to formulate their messages and reach out to customers are now able to be much more selective in deciding who to target with what messages when. And they are now making much more informed predictions as to what specific customers and prospects will do next – and what they, in turn, should do to make the most of that knowledge."

**Emotional Intelligence**

Technology is enabling a significantly shorter cycle for creating and implementing campaigns. What used to take weeks can be done in a few hours today. The careful analysis of market segments provides for much smarter communications and for your brand to become emotionally intelligent in relating to your customers. Multi-channel connections can be orchestrated to maintain consistency and continuity.

The underlying data though must be of sufficient quality or you are building a house of cards. There are basic laws to understand in managing data before automating your communications with customers.

## Garbage In = Garbage Out

"Cleanliness is next to Godliness" when maintaining data for the successful rollout of marketing automation processes.

## Analysis Paralysis

Understanding the data is important, so having expert analysts will help you make the right decisions. However, keep an open mind and be willing to creatively test new approaches. You cannot expect immediate results or you may miss out on long term opportunity.

## Averages are Dangerous

Remember that one size does not fit all, so offer variability and some level of customization when leading customers down paths in the journey they are being offered to take with your brand.

## **Automated Enthusiasm: Wine Enthusiast Case Study**

Heather Fletcher, senior editor of Target Marketing magazine, shared results from Wine Enthusiast's marketing automation campaigns. "Triggered email accounts for just 2 percent of Wine Enthusiast's email volume, but 25 percent of its email revenue," she said. "That 2 percent is also outperforming the company's previous efforts by 31 times." Glenn Edelman, Wine Enthusiast's vice president of e-commerce said: "When you get a lot more relevant, it works."

Wine Enthusiast offers a wide range of products and services to a legion of fans through print and online resources. The company partnered with Bluecore in 2013 to enhance triggered email marketing. "We wanted to get more personalized," Edelman said. "Sending emails based upon products purchased, products viewed, products abandoned – it just wasn't as simple for us to do. That's why we wanted to outsource to a market leader...to give more relevant emails to our customers...we're sending less, but generating more."

## Keeping It REAL

Personalization of content at scale, and smart engagement with prospects based on the way they interact with content, sits at the core of marketing automation. Marketing technology is a key component for companies in maintaining customer identity throughout the customer experience. Creating genuine real time interactions depends on the ability for data to seamlessly intersect along the customer journey. Customers are more empowered than ever before and are demanding their needs be met with authentic, intelligent business relationships.

## Marketing and Customer Care™ are Closely Linked

Harvard Business School Professor Theodore Levitt is referred to as a "legend in the field of marketing." He taught that companies exist for two reasons: marketing and innovation.

In 1960 he published the article, *Marketing Myopia*, where he made his now famous statement that "Marketing is a stepchild" in most corporations because of an overemphasis on creating and selling products. "But selling is not marketing," he wrote. "[Selling] is not concerned with the values that the exchange is all about. And it does not, as marketing invariably does, view the entire business process as consisting of a tightly integrated effort to discover, create, arouse, and satisfy customer needs."

Professor Levitt argued that companies and entire industries declined because management defined their businesses too narrowly. The key question that all managers must be able to answer, he advised, is "What business are you in?" The railroads, for example, "let others take customers away from them because they assumed themselves to be in the railroad business instead of the transportation business."

He also wrote, *The Marketing Imagination* where he stated, "Differentiation is the essence of everything; everything can be and is differentiable, even such 'commodities' as steel, cement, money, chemicals, and grain. The marketing imagination is the starting point of success in marketing. It is distinguished from other forms of imagination by the unique insights it brings to understanding customers, their problems, and the means to capture their attention and their custom."

**The Authors Define Marketing in Four Simple Words: *Generate Qualified Sales Leads***

**Likewise, Sales Should Be Defined as: *Take the Sales Leads Generated from Marketing and Convert them to Customers***

Marketing automation implemented properly can help make the process repeatable. This is now possible due to the widespread availability of marketing software solutions.

"There has always been a scientific aspect to marketing," says Jamie Beckland, vice president of marketing and product at 10-year-old multichannel customer identity management platform Janrain. "But marketing is probably the most artful of business disciplines. At the same time, there's clearly a push toward bringing more science and more accountability to marketing."

Worldwide, the marketing software arena was worth more than $20 billion last year and is forecast to reach more than $32 billion in 2018, according to a recent blog by Scott Brinker, who headed up the MarTech event in San Francisco earlier this year. An October article by CIO magazine indicated that at least 3,000 companies now offer what's become known as martech – or marketing technology – solutions.

According to Peter Bernstein, senior editor of tmcnet.com, "For the past few years, C-level executives have said that improving the customer experience is a top priority. Yet they have really only paid lip service to the concept. This has been well-documented in numerous surveys and books. In fact, the fastest growing C-level job titles globally are positions such as 'Chief Customer Experience Officer'. The limiting factor seems to be that their responsibilities are ill-defined and they don't seem to have clout, especially when it comes to settling territorial issues between IT, operations and marketing. Thanks to social media, marketing controls a massive and growing part of customer experience technology budgets and recommendations."

Steve:

""A few days after registering online for the Spring 2015 Cleveland Half-Marathon on Active.com, I received an email announcing a One Day ONLY Sale on Hoka One One brand running shoes. Through the intuitive use of my data, I was identified as someone ready to train for the race and likely to need new shoes. Actually I had been anticipating a purchase of Hoka One One shoes as some of my friends had already bought a pair for themselves. My delay was the $170 price tag. So, when I saw the ad for a One Day ONLY Sale on $170 Hoka One One shoes for just $90, I immediately placed my order. I absolutely love these shoes. They really are the most comfortable running shoes I have ever worn. They make me feel like I am running on pillows. And guess what? I will buy them again in the future even if I have to pay $170. I tell everyone about my experience and the great deal I received."

"Imagine if they took this one step further with their marketing automation."

"Why not offer me information and content on tips to train and prepare for the race? They could invite me to a webinar or to download a white paper or e-book. A mobile app opportunity is certainly something that lends itself to a good fit in this situation."

"That would TAKE ME, the CUSTOMER, to the NEXT LEVEL.""

*Taking Your Customer Care™ to the Next Level*

Loews Miami Beach Hotel uses marketing automation to enhance the Customer Care™ experience. At check-in, customers are asked to provide their mobile number and for consent to send a text message when your room is ready. You can go to the pool, have lunch and relax until you get the alert. There's no reason to watch your phone and worry about not hearing the phone ring to receive notification. The hotel also sends a mobile survey the following day to gauge your level of happiness with the check-in experience.

Restaurants could create an opportunity to text your server, or receive a text when your table is ready. Nearly every business can provide benefit to consumers with the appropriate use of marketing automation technologies. Companies should consider offering two-way texting, allowing customers to request assistance and provide feedback.

Wall Street is also paying attention as companies are spending billions in the aggregate on marketing automation applications and methodologies.

Ad Age Report: Marketing Automation

"It's about engaging customers on any channel or device with an orchestrated approach based on data," said Gordon Evans, vice president of product marketing at Salesforce.com's ExactTarget Marketing Cloud, which offers marketing-automation software.

The power of these platforms has turned them into attractive acquisition targets for software behemoths like Adobe, IBM, Oracle, and Salesforce, which have all snatched up at least one marketing-automation company in the past two years. When connected with other software platforms, such as CRM, a marketing automation system can make an entire organization more effective in the way it communicates with prospects and customers. The practice is already popular with B2B marketers, but the tools are being used by B2C marketers as well.

## Marketing Automation and Video

Marketing and advertising are obviously two great use cases for video, which adds up to better results for the companies using it. "Open rates on emails that have subject lines noting they include video have a 55 percent higher click through rate than the average email," says Amy Hyde, director of technology alliances at Brightcove.

According to Qumu, 64 percent of viewers are more likely to buy a product after watching a video. They recommend going beyond product videos to bring an immediate, personal touch to any event or campaign by creating a video and sharing it with prospects or existing customers.

You've probably heard of Meerkat, a live-streaming video app built on top of Twitter. While Meerkat isn't a platform designed specifically for businesses, as it is more of a social mobile app, many businesses are using it to promote customer engagement. Meerkat community manager Ryan Cooley says: "People want authenticity. Community is about allowing for exchange, and video can do that really well."

The team at Qumu profess that video is becoming more essential for online communications all the time, a fact that businesses can't ignore. The company recommends using "unpolished" video to create conversation that feels legitimate rather than staged, such as:

- Testimonials
- Live Webcasts and Product Demos
- Company Created Content
- Thank You Messages to Employees and Customers

For example, Meerkat is becoming popular with real estate professionals looking to conduct virtual open houses for listings on the market. Just like celebrities and members of the media, brands are quickly discovering the potential of using apps like Meerkat to offer more access and transparency.

Live video sharing on social platforms is here to stay, as evidenced by Twitter's decision to acquire a similar live-streaming app called Periscope. Unlike Meerkat videos, Periscope videos start automatically without asking you to log into Twitter for the live feed. These two competing services are expected to battle it out for some time, but with the engineering, marketing and recruiting resources of a large public company like Twitter behind it, Periscope certainly has the edge.

"Despite a history of false starts, live video chat for eCommerce and customer support is now at the beginning of a viable adoption cycle," Forrester writes in a promotion for its 2014 study on the topic. "Early adopters — most notably Amazon — are plowing ahead. A handful of firms have been using B2C video chat for up to two years — some with very encouraging returns."

## Starbucks Video Barista

Starbucks has implemented video chat technology at some of its stores for drive thru ordering. It is designed for customers who love the ability to see a real live person take their order yet prefer not to leave their car. Initial comments from customers indicate the drive thru experience becomes friendlier and more personable.

## Amazon Mayday Button

Amazon pioneered a move toward video-centric service with its Mayday Button. Introduced in September 2014, it allows customers to push a button on their Kindle Fire HDX tablet to immediately initiate a video-conferencing session with a live agent. The service was so well received that, according to Amazon, 75 percent of Kindle Fire HDX users now use Mayday to engage with the company's service representatives.

## How Do You Generate Qualified Sales Leads? Your Company will DIE if you are Not Creating Qualified Leads

One of the most important aspects of lead generation is having a good inbound marketing strategy. The first step is figuring out a strategy; what will be the public face of your inbound marketing, and what kind of content will be relevant to your leads? What kind of publication schedule should be put in place, what will be the web site platform for this marketing effort?

The next step is designing a website with clear 'call to action' buttons or links. The point of the inbound marketing is lead generation, so the content on the site should not get in the way of actually generating these leads; it needs to be obvious how readers can take the next step.

That next step is creating good inbound marketing content. An easy way to figure out what type of content to offer up is to see what questions your audience is asking and then answer those questions. This often is the difference between viral posts and those that are more or less ignored.

It also helps to connect with larger Web publications that can expand your reach. Reach out to editors at these publications and see what they need. You might just have ideas and content they would want to publish.

Just as important as having the right content is constantly adjusting the plan. Your inbound marketing strategy should include regular review to see what is working and what is not. You should keep daily, weekly and monthly tracking, and then adjust weekly or monthly based on the data you have collected.

### Be Authentic to Your Brand

Customers love authentic companies. They like it when a company has a strong and clear message and that message is consistent across all of their marketing platforms. So, don't try and be everything to everyone. Customers want the experts and the company that is the best in their industry. Focus on communicating that through your branding and your conversion rates will go up, resulting in more leads.

Understanding and effectively implementing the basic principles of marketing will differentiate your company. Your customers will be more committed and loyal to your brand and you will be a clear and present danger to your competitors.

**One of the first things the bean counters begin to cut from the budget when facing an economic downturn is marketing.**

<u>This is exactly the opposite strategy business should be implementing in this scenario</u>. In a lean environment, you must reinforce your leadership position, and enhance your marketing and Customer Care™ processes to GAIN MARKET SHARE. This is another way you can *Take Your Customer Care™ to the Next Level!*

For more detailed information and practical guidance on how to successfully hire and develop your marketing team and implement industry leading marketing strategies, refer to the upcoming book by the authors, ***Taking Your Marketing Strategy to the Next Level*™**.

## Chapter Four

# BUSINESS IS PERSONAL: ONE TO ONE MARKETING LEADS TO CUSTOMER ENGAGEMENT AND RETENTION

The days of mass marketing are behind us. **Henry Ford's Model T "came in any color as long as it was black."** Today the customer chooses the color of the exterior, interior and the trim. We crave unique, individualized experiences, as varied as our personal preferences and tastes. One size fits all will not cut it anymore.

Keeping customers engaged, happy, and spending is the result of loyalty marketing. Delivering relevant and engaging content will increase customer lifetime value and overall revenue for the business.

### What's That Smell? Your R.O.T. Content

**R:** Redundant
**O:** Outdated
**T:** Trivial

Digital Marketing Depot presented a recent webinar led by Ethology. They reinforced, "Website visitors and search engines love fresh, relevant content. You know what they hate? The Redundant, Outdated, and Trivial (R.O.T.) content that's sitting on your site right now."

Show You Care with your Content: Keep your content fresh and relevant to encourage your customers to hang out online with you and develop a deeper relationship with you.

**It Costs up to 10 Times more to Attract New Customers than it does to Retain Existing Ones**

Customer retention is more than just keeping customers. You have to make them happy with a reason to tell others about your business, buy more of the same products, buy new product categories, buy higher margin products, and increase the frequency of their visits.

Build a two-way relationship with customers. Predictive analytics provides in depth customer insights to drive engagement through personalization.

**75 percent of U.S. consumers like it when companies personalize messaging and offers so they are more relevant, according to Accenture Interactive.**

**41% percent of U.S. consumers buy when they receive personalized emails, according to The e-tailing group.**

Yet 70 percent of brands do not personalize their email. Putting your customers' names in the subject line of emails is just the first step. Send updated information based on your customers' known preferences.

Steve:

"I absolutely love the Sonos brand wireless speaker systems and subscribe to Rhapsody music service for our household. The company sends us regular email updates announcing new music available from those artists and styles of music we choose most often."

## Do You Know Your Customer?

<u>Demographic, Transactional, and Psychographic Data</u>

Demographic information – such as address, age, gender, and income – has been used for the better part of the past century to relate with customers of various backgrounds.

Transactional data involves the specific interactions I have had with a company, ranging from touch points to actual purchases.

Psychographic data is information on things I like to do, where I like to go and what I like to buy. It's information on how I spend my money including what magazines, TV shows, music, books, and apps I order, download, etc.

When demographic, transactional and psychographic data are all combined, we can more easily pull the pieces of the puzzle together and truly know the customer. We know where they live, what they like to do and what they've bought from us.

<u>Putting Data into Context</u>

Next we need to know about the current state of our customers – what they are experiencing right now. Adding context helps identify if they have had any change in their lives, such as a marriage, or a death in the family. It can also reveal the weather in their city, whether they are on a trip, what they are saying online. You are now able to integrate this knowledge with analytics solutions to personalize the experience and journey with your company.

Consider the business context as well for B2B interactions. Has their organization just completed a merger? Are they introducing a new product? Have they received recent press coverage, etc.?

## Appreciate Customers' Personal Values

Julie Lyons, president and COO of Zenzi Communications, explains the importance of understanding our customers' values. She states: "Demographics and psychographics are part of the equation. When we understand the inner motivations and values of our customers, we gain a deeper understanding of what inspires their purchase decisions."

"Values don't just tell us who is making the decision, but why they are making it."

Julie goes on to explain: "In the field of psychology, values are defined as the goals and beliefs that guide our actions and behavior. Values motivate how each of us thinks, feels, reacts and communicates. For most of us, our values tend to stay constant over time, even through major life changes. Values are the 'non-negotiables.' Values are not just broad, abstract concepts. They can be tied to specific behaviors with the right analysis. Think of values as the drivers of people's decisions. For example, when looking at the wall of yogurt in the dairy aisle, which one do we choose, and why? Do we choose one because it's on sale, or because it's organic? Or maybe it's the brand that our mom always bought?"

Each individual is unique in the way they determine what is of most value to them and their decision making reflects their values. Organizations now and in the future which care enough to connect with their customers personally on a deeper emotional level will have the greatest long-term success.

## Data Quality

Data quality refers to the reliability, completeness, and accuracy of information flowing through your systems. Pay attention in your organization to the ways data is created, modified, combined, calculated, reported, cleansed, and retained. Take responsibility for the accuracy, consistency and completeness of your data.

According to Informatica: "The hallmark of data quality is how well data supports the context in which it's consumed. Driving data quality requires a repeatable process that includes:

- Defining the specific requirements for 'good data'
- Establishing rules for certifying the quality of that data
- Appointing a responsible team member to manage your data process and maintain accountability
- Integrating those rules into an existing workflow to both test and allow for exception handling, and
- Continuing to monitor and measure data quality during its lifecycle"

**And the Survey Says...**

The 7th Annual "Personalization Consumer Survey" was released in 2015 by MyBuys and e-tailing group. Results of the survey indicate that 53 percent of consumers feel it's important for retailers to recognize them as the same person across all channels and devices used to shop. And 48 percent say they purchase more from retailers that leverage interests and buying behaviors to personalize the customer experience across all touch points.

With regards to purchasing, 53 percent say they spend more with retailers that make website product recommendations based on browsing or buying behaviors, and 52 percent say the same about targeting through behavior-based online ads. However, just under half (48 percent) say they spend more with retailers that send personalized emails.

Still, personalization can cut both ways:

- 39 percent of consumers say they get frustrated when retailers don't offer personalized website recommendations.

- 38 percent say the same about personalized email offers.
- 37 percent express angst when their online purchases aren't considered.
- 34 percent feel the same way about ignored in-store purchases when receiving subsequent marketing offers.

Personalization is more important to those ages 25 to 34. Sixty-nine percent of this age group said they are comfortable sharing their information with retailers to improve their shopping experience, while only 46 percent of those ages 55 and older feel the same.

Personalization is critical across all touch points, mobile included. Twenty percent of consumers claim tablets as their primary online shopping tool, according to the study, and 18 percent say they strictly use smartphones. Also, the report recommends personalization across all touch points because 70 percent of 25- to 34-year-old shoppers research products or make purchases across at least three devices.

Personalization should go beyond online shopping. More than half of consumers say retailers who consider their in-store purchases offer a superior shopping experience across all online channels. And nearly 80 percent are also willing to allow retailers to use information from their in-store purchases to provide a more personalized experience whenever they shop.

Analyze transactional history to develop customer profiles, leading to personalized offers such as escalated discounts or free shipping for those who have lapsed in frequency.

Create a single source of customer data from information across web, social, mobile, email, phone, or in-store channels. Organize the data into your customer profiles to offer personalized experiences and to predict customer behaviors. Recommending relevant products to customers based on their profiles leads to increased engagement and more timely purchase decisions.

Amazon has led the way and consumers now expect this when shopping online.

**39 percent of U.S. consumers buy more when products are suggested based on past buying behavior, according to The e-tailing group.**

**54 percent of retailers that utilized product recommendations increased average order value year over year, according to Forrester Research.**

**Enable Customers to Make Your Brand Their Own**

Owned by Nike, Converse sneakers recently launched the Made by You campaign celebrating the 100th anniversary of Chuck Taylor All-Star shoes. Converse was once worn by nearly 90 percent of NBA players. Today the brand is hugely popular with many different age groups, from Millennials to Baby Boomers.

Steve:

"My teenage daughters wear Converse sneakers as does a friend who is nearing retirement."

The Made by You campaign enables customers to design their own personalized shoes starting from what the company refers to as a "Blank Canvas." Converse brand lovers share stories on social media and post photos of their own shoes along with their personal thoughts. The campaign extends the Converse story into an individualized experience.

**Your Very Own Coca-Cola**

The Share a Coke campaign in the summer of 2014 offered unexpected personalization. We can all relate to the exciting feeling when you find your name spelled correctly in a store with customized key chains, coffee mugs, etc.

**Steve:**

"My daughters' names are Elise and Elizabeth. When they were younger, they would both search the displays for personalized trinkets. Of course, Elizabeth would nearly always find her name, but Elise rarely did. Whenever we happened to by chance find something with Elise's name spelled exactly right, we always purchased it and she would display it proudly in her room. We even ordered custom name products for both girls a few times so they could both have their names represented."

Share a Coke captured this excitement, creating a personalized brand experience for Coca-Cola customers around the nation by printing individual names and phrases on Coke bottles and cans throughout the country. Combining personalization with social media, customers created their own experiences to share with the world.

Coke had been in a steady 10-year sales decline, but this campaign made a difference.

Prior to the campaign launch, Coke's year-over-year sales trend with 20-ounce bottles were about even with Pepsi's sales. Once the summer kicked off, Coke began producing bottles and cans with personalized names and phrases printed on the labels.

Shoppers responded and throughout the campaign, Coke sales skyrocketed as compared to Pepsi. People were not only buying Cokes with their name listed, but they also purchased those inscribed with the names of friends and family members. Consumers literally searched for familiar names and took photos to share on social media, creating a viral sensation.

**Are your Customers Bored with You?**

When was the last time you reached out to your customers to provide them with information or tools to help them in their everyday lives? Is your communication the same with weekly or monthly advertisements that look and feel the same? Do customers only connect with you when they are looking to buy?

You should stay on the mind of customers by being a resource to them and relating to their needs. For example, food brands can do that by providing recipes and new ways to use their products. Lifestyle brands can do it by promoting health and wellness programs. Home improvement brands can create customer interaction forums to share ideas. Nonprofit organizations can offer one-to-one connections for relational support when dealing with a family member who is ill.

Analyst Gerry Moran of MarketingThink points out that what a company is selling should be positioned from a concierge standpoint – how can your products or services help the end user do their job better or live their life better.

"They want to be educated on how your stuff can help them – then they will buy," said Moran. "The Home Depot builds a great customer experience by giving away their expertise during their Do-It-Yourself, Do-It-Herself and Kids Workshops and, Stitch-Fix, the woman's subscription clothes service, presents possibilities by providing custom combinations printed on in-box instructions."

By providing helpful resources to the public at large, your value will be perceived beyond the transactional nature of the purchases of only your customers.

## Communicating with Distracted Customers

According to a 2013 Responsys survey, the average length of time consumers will pay attention to your online communications is just 30 seconds! That leaves very little time to stay connected and engaged with your audience. Clearly a personalized and relevant experience is necessary to maintain visibility with customers. One size fits all mass communications tend to be ignored with competition from competing media sources. Distractions will only increase as the digital age progresses and dual screen multi-tasking becomes the norm.

**Seasonal Strategies**

Each year, marketers look forward to seasonal promotions to create an increase in sales. According to James Green, CEO of search retargeting leader Magnetic, "prior to each event — whether it's the Super Bowl, Mother's Day or Back-to-School — search and site activity send strong signals of buying intent, which is critical to new customer acquisition and retention. Understanding how, when and where your customers are searching around seasonal events can trigger phenomenal results and put marketers at a clear advantage."

**Customer Care™ Must be a Priority for Your Business**

Most everyone would agree that taking care of customers is necessary to stay in business. Then why are so few organizations successfully implementing *Next Level Customer Care™*?

Convenience, Differentiation, Diminished Churn, Loyalty, Quality of Service, Retention, and Value are the buzzwords today. Decision makers must develop a coordinated data analytics solution to capture data from all service channels. By carefully analyzing information from the myriad of customer interactions, predictive models determine where improvements are needed and will be most effective. When this intelligence is applied strategically, the ultimate result will be an improved service approach going forward.

Understanding your customers' intrinsic needs and wants through a systematic approach involving data and marketing analytics will help you *Take Your Customer Relationships to the Next Level*.

## Chapter Five

# THE CAREFUL TREATMENT OF CUSTOMERS RESULTS IN CUSTOMER RETENTION

The infamous Ed Debevic's restaurant in Chicago has a tradition of mistreating customers for theatrical effect. Its trademarked phrase, "Eat and Get Out" does not engender loyalty except in the context of a well-played performance. Most businesses do not have that luxury and must treat the customer with the utmost of respect and care.

**Customer "Depreciation"**

Do you and your employees show appreciation to your customers or do they become a depreciating asset in your portfolio? Making customers feel appreciated, comfortable, and satisfied is the way to prevent customers from feeling you are "indifferent" to them.

**68 percent of customers who leave do so because of a company employee's indifference,** according to Dr. Michael LeBoeuf in *How to Win Customers and Keep Them for Life.*

Many businesses assume employees already know how to provide decent customer service. They believe customers are in the store seeking a product and nothing more. Research proves this assumption incorrect. While it is true that most customers enter a business looking for a particular item, the quality of their experience during the transaction determines if they will return.

The actions and attitudes of the employees who interact with a customer leaves an indelible impression of the company. The impression of employees—the receptionist, the salesperson, but also those behind the scenes—can be more important than the merchandise for customer retention. Shopping at its essence is an interactive and immersing experience.

According to Richard Gerson, author of <u>Beyond Customer Service: Keeping Customers for Life</u>: "Customer service is governed by the rule of 10s: If it costs $10,000 to get a new customer, it takes only 10 seconds to lose him or her and 10 years for the customer to get over it." It doesn't have to be difficult. You start by being nice and making sure the people who represent your brand are also being nice to your customers.

## Can I Get that "Thank YOU" in Writing?

When was the last time you sent a personalized Thank YOU note or card to your customers? The little things matter, as they say. Take time out to send personalized notes and cards. You can do this yourself as a small business, and larger companies have the ability to use a variety of service providers to create memorable thank you cards and gifts.

## Culture-Driven Customer Care™

Create a culture for employees to pay close attention to customers' needs. Select employees and help them develop these skills:

- Maintain Eye Contact
- Listen Carefully
- Don't Take Calls While Interacting with Customers
- Be Relaxed...Don't Appear Time Pressured
- Show Compassion and Empathy
- Treat All Customers Equally Regardless of Transaction Size

## Treat Customers as People and Not Numbers on a Spreadsheet

Billing departments are notorious for less than friendly communications with your valued customers. Melissa Kovacevic from Intradiem's *Real-Time Frontline* blog shared an email sent by an accounting clerk at a major hotel chain a month after a hotel stay. The customer was a frequent travel member with this chain and thought this might be a scam email based on what was written. He had to call to confirm it was really from this hotel:

<u>"I am writing to inform you that during your stay at the (hotel), your bill was left unsettled.... The MasterCard did not swipe correctly and is coming up as invalid. Please fill out the credit card authorization attached to settle your account"</u>

No salutation, no cordial greeting, no thanks for your business and then a request to email personal information to a stranger a month after the hotel stay. Clearly no understanding how a customer would feel receiving such a cold and strange message that ended up causing more work for the customer.

## Walk in the Customers Shoes

How would you react? How would the average person understand what we are offering? Design the business process around what is most convenient for customers and not just the business departments.

Ask employees to share customer experiences, needs and feelings, and how they interacted or created a positive effect on the customer.

## Companies that Make their Customers Feel Special Get to Keep Them

Phone interactions can be as engaging as greeting a customer personally face to face provided the agent is focusing on the person on the other end of the line and not just on the screen or script in front of them. It is not only what you say, but how you say it that makes the difference. Being friendly and authentic goes a long way.

**By 2020, Customer Experience Will Overtake Price and Product as the Key Brand Differentiator, according to Walker, *Customers 2020: The Future of...Customer Experience***

**Create Concierge Level Service in EVERY Customer Interaction**

The Concierge at Luxury Hotel brands are your direct link to specialized service...the position is designed to satisfy every guest's needs, wants and whims. Our Customer Care™ should be delivered in a level to the degree of a concierge.

Nadji:

"When I lived and studied in France years ago, I noticed that every apartment building had a concierge on the first floor. The concierge was not appreciated as much as today in the U.S. The concierge was nosy, read all the mail and knew what everyone was doing."

Being a bit nosy about your customer today is essential to deliver personalized Customer Care™.

**Effortless Experiences**

According to Dixon, Toman, and DeLisi in their book, *The Effortless Experience,* the more effort your customers invest to resolve an issue, the less likely they are to remain loyal to your business. Go to your website now and try to find simple answers to basic questions. Do the search results require knowing and using certain keywords? Are multiple answers offered requiring the customer to wade through each choice before moving forward? You may be surprised by the amount of work your customers have to do simply to do business with you.

## A State of "Bliss"

The word bliss is defined as "a state of perfect happiness, typically so as to be oblivious of everything else." We obviously want our customers to be happy and oblivious of our competitors. But how do we do it? Rik Reppe, advisory partner with PwC, recommends creating "bliss points" in the customer experience with your brand.

Reppe says: "Create more 'bliss points,' experiences that stand out in a customer's mind, while minimizing the pain points. Some fixes will be obvious—for example, instructing the receptionist in a physician's waiting room to make eye contact with patients as they check in. Others are more subtle and often more complex, requiring operational realignment or restructuring, or broader cultural change throughout an organization. Focus on the bliss points that provide the greatest customer value relative to your own strategic objectives and their impact on revenue and profitability."

## Emotional Engagement

Individualize and personalize the experience. Everyone perceives a transaction uniquely. Perception is the driving factor in the way customers evaluate their experience with a company. It may or not even be factual, but perception becomes the customer's reality.

Consumer perception is selective by nature. Selective exposure is the act of limiting the type and amount of information that is received and admitted to the awareness of the consumer. It allows them to select only the information that interests them and is consistent with their feelings and beliefs. Selective retention is the act of remembering only the information we want to remember. Selective distortion involves the customer practice of distorting incoming messages so they are more consistent with their existing mind-set.

## For a Customer, How They See the Issue is More Important than How You See the Issue.

### Engagement Analytics

Heavily siloed, customer engagement data is often disjointed and doesn't give marketers, sales professionals, and customer service representatives a holistic view of the customer journey. Verint Engagement Analytics is a cloud-based solution that captures customer, employee, transaction, and interaction data, and makes it accessible in a single unified view. The solution can take data from all channels into account, including web and mobile activity, phone interactions, emails, chats, secure messages, case notes, social media messages, desktop activity, employee performance, and survey responses.

### Great Customer Experience Drives Profitability

"If companies reduced their customer deflection rate by just 5 percent, then profitability would increase by 25 to 125 percent," said Karyn Dupree of BPA Quality. Many companies believe they offer excellent service, but clearly there is a huge disconnect as only 1 percent of customers feel their needs are consistently being met, according to *Forbes* magazine.

Steve:

"Have you ever visited a retail store and left with a hunch that they wouldn't stay in business? My teenage daughters were attracted to Delia's, a trendy fashion store and catalog. Nearly every time we placed an order the store would be out of whatever blouse or other item they wanted to order. There would be a several month delay and when the product finally arrived, the season had changed. Then one day we visited the mall store together. The rack pricing signs were deceiving. $29.99 and up was advertised, but there was nothing on the rack left at the price listed. Guess what? The retailer closed its doors. It did not treat customers with care. I knew it, and clearly many others had the same experience."

We can go back in time and remember several distinct company brands that were iconic for their influence in the past, yet today they are just a memory.

### Oldsmobile

The company was famous for developing the first car to feature automatic transmission.

However, when General Motors restructured early this century, Oldsmobile was sacked along with these other well-known GM brands – such as Hummer, Pontiac, Saab, and Saturn.

### Montgomery Ward

This business was the first to create a catalog with more than 10,000 pages.

Threatened by discount retailers such as Kmart, Target and Walmart, Montgomery Ward lost popularity and closed in 2000.

### Blockbuster

You know the story well. Streaming killed the video star. Although Blockbuster had its chance to purchase Netflix in 2000 for the bargain price of $50 million...those were the days!

### Kodak and Polaroid

Although Polaroid Instant film is still popular with the vintage set, digital photography and mobile technology made the core businesses of these once stalwart companies obsolete.

Adapting to change and understanding what the customer wants is the number one rule of corporate survival today! In other words, make the product the customer wants and give it to them with outstanding Customer Care™.

## Customer Engagement Drives Growth

Engaged customers are usually better advocates of the brand and are more loyal and more profitable, according to research by Gartner. "All organizations in the private and public sector connect with customers, most often through the work of the marketing, sales and customer service departments," said Michael Maoz, vice president and distinguished analyst at Gartner. "However, in most cases, these organizations are not actually engaging with the customer, and instead they have been disengaging for a decade in order to lower costs. Furthermore, relatively few have an enterprise wide approach to engaging with customers."

## Customer Care™ Common Sense: Create Positive Experiences

When dealing with customers, nothing seals the deal more than a good experience. After all, engaging customers in good experiences is what keeps them coming back for more.

According to Noble Systems, in the CMO Council's *Giving Customer Voice More Volume* survey, 83 percent of the executives surveyed said that the customer experience is "essential" or "increasingly important" in driving brand advocacy and business performance.

And in Forrester Research's The State of Customer Experience report, 90 percent of respondents said customer experience is "very important" or "critical" to their firms' strategy. Forrester's 2012 The Emerging Role of Social Customer Experience in Customer Care study shows that, while the phone remains the most important channel for 88 percent of companies, 74 percent of respondents indicated that improving the cross-channel customer experience was a major objective.

## Employee Alignment with Customer Engagement

Recruit employees for service roles who will win the hearts and minds of your customers. They must be very good listeners and be able to provide information in a concise, professional and timely manner.

**Walt Disney: "You can design and create, and build the most wonderful place in the world. But it takes people to make the dream a reality."**

Create an environment that moves beyond mediocrity. <u>In the eyes of average people, average is always considered outstanding.</u> Exceptional people expect exceptional service experiences.

## Enable Employees to Make the RIGHT Choices

Make each and every customer experience strong. For every customer complaint, there are likely 25 or more unhappy customers who will not share their frustration. Envision has reported that customers are four times more likely to reach out to a direct competitor if a problem they experience is service related as opposed to product or price related.

**Policies must be understood. Don't wait for employees to ask the purpose of a certain task, tell them why you do it and solicit their input along the way, so they buy into the process.**

## Make a List and Check It Twice

Document what needs to be done for your team. Checklists are essential to ensure consistency with your brand experience. Every time a customer chooses to engage with your business there should be an expectation of excellent service, positive environment and friendly interaction.

## Test Your Process

The only way you can be sure your process is working is to test it out personally. Many organizations have designed elaborate mystery shopper programs. Third-party services are also available. Owners of every business large or small must be in tune with the pulse of the customer experience. What happens when you walk into your store with a question, request assistance online, or call your own call center? Are you delighted by the way your staff handles customer inquiries? If not, then your customers clearly are not pleased either.

## Recognize the Behaviors that Delight Customers

Never let them see you sweat. We all have tough days, personal crises, and unexpected setbacks in our daily lives. Show by example and encourage your team to relax, take a deep breath and not let the stress show to the customer or other employees. If you treat your employees as partners in the business, then they will know you respect them and their personal lives.

## "Wham, Bam, Thank You..."

If average transaction time is the metric you reinforce above all else, don't be surprised when customers feel rushed, pressured, uncomfortable and less than satisfied.

Rich Tehrani successfully predicted the future back in January 2001 with his editorial, titled, *Après Moi Le Deluge: or Click, Bam... Thank You, Ma'am*. Here is an excerpt:

""In November, I discussed how those of us who would be conducting e-commerce transactions during the 2000 holiday season would need to do a much better job of providing service than what occurred during the 1999 holiday season. Judging by the positive response I received regarding that column, many agreed."

"It is rough to believe that less than a year ago, it seemed that pure dot com companies were guaranteed runaway success stories. You remember the logic: brick and mortar meant overhead and overhead meant decreased profits."

"The media gave a lot of attention to e-commerce startups, thus working for these companies became much sexier than any other job opportunity available. Whenever you couple a sexy company with the potential to rapidly become a millionaire, you're sure to have the best talent flocking to you. So dot coms seemed invincible: They were flush with investment cash, they had stock prices that consistently headed northward and they had the ability to sell additional shares at will to raise more capital."

"But what about all the e-commerce companies that got flushed when the dot com bubble burst? It is my belief that many of these companies would still be around, and others would be doing considerably better, if they simply went about their business differently. A great deal of these sites took tremendous amounts of money and devoted these funds to advertising and website design, figuring that it was all they needed to do. In hindsight, this was a huge gamble. They figured live customer help wasn't needed; after all, their customers would be shopping on the web, so why would they ever want to speak to a human being? These customers could just use self-help web-based systems...perhaps a FAQ section was all that was needed. Anything more, like being able to (heaven-forbid) contact a live, breathing being would be sacrilegious and would defeat the whole purpose of using the Internet, right? They couldn't have been more wrong."

"They thought interaction centers were a thing of the past and all that was needed was a flashy website and the thrill and convenience of e-commerce would guarantee the success of their site. Who needs to call and speak to a live person on the web? They were wrong again!"

"While these companies were delivering lackluster service to their customers, and turning them off in the process, the dot com world was exploding with competition as the barrier to entry was minimal and venture capital flowed like Niagara Falls. Survival of the fittest is not just a law of nature: it now also applies to dot com companies. The healthiest companies will emerge -- battered and bruised, but alive."

"In the wake of tremendous tech turmoil on Wall Street, it seems that those brick-and-mortars (you remember, the companies that were doomed just over a year ago) certainly look like they will do very well as commerce moves to the Internet. These companies have the added advantage of integrating e-commerce into their existing channels. These more traditional companies have an understanding of their customers and business plans that are built to last."

"The companies that are doing it right and are embracing the web and adding the latest technology to satisfy their customers will have a huge advantage over their dot com counterparts. They know that shoppers still want personal service, any way they choose to contact the company. They understand that one of the communications channels customers still want to choose is walking into a store and talking face-to-face with a salesperson. They also understand that by integrating their brick-and-mortar and Internet presence, they will offer the best of all worlds."

"It is my sincere wish that companies begin to place more emphasis on pleasing their customers, and I hope that Tehrani's Law of Customer Service helps quantify why we all need to provide our customers with the best customer service in the 21$^{st}$ century.""

## Give your Customers the "White Glove Treatment"

Nadji:

""When I was invited to speak at a global Customer Care™ conference in Japan with my beautiful wife, Julie, a few years back, I noticed the cab drivers were all wearing white gloves. The cab drivers were extremely polite and helpful. In fact, nearly everyone we met on our two-week trip went out of their way to care for us and made our experience memorable. My wife, Julie, spent quite a bit of time touring while I was in meetings."

"As we were approaching the end of our stay, the leader of the host group asked if there was anything we missed or were not able to experience. Julie expressed she had wanted to find a kimono in a certain color but was unable to find one. This man, to our surprise, contacted a custom tailor to design and create a kimono in her size and color choice. He presented it to Julie in a nicely wrapped package at 8 a.m. the following morning on our way to the airport. I was amazed, Julie was delighted, and we left with a feeling of complete satisfaction. The people we interacted with truly traveled the extra mile to create an unmatched Customer Care™ experience for us. We will never forget their kindness to us.""

**Do your customers remember their experiences with your company fondly? Do they tell everyone they meet even years later?**

Be Clear and Consistent

We entrust our relationship with our customers with our employees. Do we trust our employees to delight our customers? The quality of the customer experience depends on your team members' performance. Make sure you have invested in the people and processes to enable a smooth, efficient experience for your employees. Your customers' experiences will mirror that.

## Create a Culture of Engagement

Don MacPherson, president and co-founder of Modern Survey explains that organizations working to create a culture of engagement need to set very clear expectations that employees need to do their best work on a regular basis. Surprisingly few companies tell candidates in the hiring process that it is their responsibility to be engaged at work.

MacPherson says: "I do a fair amount of public speaking to human resources professionals. I ask the audience for a show of hands if they believe employees should bring their best to work. About 80 percent of hands go up. Then I ask if they state that as an expectation in the interviewing process. About 5 percent of the hands go up. Setting the expectation sends a clear message to the candidate that this is a place where my leaders, co-workers and customers will routinely expect the best."

The Temkin Group published its Employee Engagement Benchmark Study, 2015, which analyzes the engagement levels of more than 5,000 U.S. employees. The company found that although employee engagement overall has increased over the past year, engagement levels still vary by organization, industry, and individual. Companies with stronger financial performances and better customer experience have employees who are considerably more engaged than their peers. Temkin researchers found that companies that outpace their competitors in customer experience (CX) have 50 percent more engaged employees than those with CX that lags their peers.

Reinforce why excellent service matters to the health and survival of the business. Show team members how they interact with each other and the customer makes the experience memorable for all.

Stef Miller at UserTesting asks the question: "Who Owns Your Company's Customer Experience?" UserTesting publishes the annual UX Industry Survey Report. Miller says: "There's a significant number of people out there who don't actually know who is ultimately responsible for the customer experience at their company! In fact, 'not knowing who owns the customer experience' was one of the top 5 responses out of over 1,600 respondents."

Miller points out that customer happiness is everyone's responsibility and offers recommendations. "If your company is filled with a bunch of 'That-Just-Isn't-My-Problem' employees, then you've got yourself a problem. Every email, every link, every checkout experience belongs to the people who design it, build it, test it, message it, and support it."

"So first, find out if everyone in your company knows how important a customer's experience is," she says. "Identify who is in charge of this—they're probably doing a whole lot of competitor benchmarking, user research, process assessment and reporting. Then, get connected! Listen to your customers, share what you learn, and continue to push for others to get involved in creating a happy place for your customers."

## A Happy Employee is a Better Employee

Create work-life balance for your team. Provide resources to encourage positive thinking, living and healthy habits. Wellness leads to better attendance and most importantly presenteeism.

What are the things your staff members have to take time off work to do, or run out at lunchtime to handle? Arrange for these services to be available directly at the workplace so employees are not wondering when and how they are going to handle all their personal time commitments.

Here is a partial list of things you can arrange to provide on-site to create an environment that boosts employee morale and shows your employees you CARE about them:

- Food services with healthy options
- Doctor visits
- Prescription delivery
- Gym memberships
- Laundry/dry cleaning service
- Childcare partnerships

**Involve employees in the decision making. They will buy into the process and take personal ownership.**

Chris Miksen of Demand Media states: "Trust serves as a key factor in determining your employee relations. Companies that make decisions while keeping employees in the dark may lose their employees' trust. Some employees may believe that the company is keeping decisions about its future plans secret because those plans include adverse outcomes for employees. By involving your employees in the company's decision making, you're bringing transparency to the workplace."

Employees should understand the metrics of success for the company and how their role impacts the bottom line. Provide quarterly financial updates to all your staff. Incentivize team members who suggest specific and tangible ways to improve profitability and customer retention. Communicate the rewards to all employees to recognize individual contributions and also to encourage further creative input from others.

**Customers expect staff to be knowledgeable, willing, and able to help them. They will return to the business again and again in the future because of the people in your business being attentive to their needs and who have the power to make routine decisions without having to defer to a supervisor.**

Staff retention leads to a stable workforce and consistent customer experience, which is a real differentiator today. Empowered employees see themselves as professionals who have careers and not as individuals who simply work 9-to-5 jobs.

## Crack the Code on Employee Engagement

How do you influence your staff so they give their maximum effort? It is NOT just about satisfaction. It is also NOT just about happiness. The key is to get your staff to CARE about your business and the people you do business with. When they do, employees become committed. They go all in voluntarily. Isn't that what you want?

## Are Employees, Your Raving Fans?

Annette Franz, vice president of customer experience at Touchpoint Dashboard, explains why employee experience must come before customer experience. "When employees have a great experience with their employers," she says, "not only does it translate to a great customer experience but also leads to employees become raving fans of the brand and of the organization."

"Because of that enthusiasm and passion for the brand, for the business, employees are eager to contribute to its success. And when we're all working together for the success of the business, ultimately, customers win, too."

## Do You Have a Dream Team? Select Your Staff Carefully

The individuals you connect directly with your customers should take the responsibility personally.

The Ingredients for Creating a *Next Level Customer Care*™ *Team:*

*You are looking for these specific qualities in your employees...*

Flexibility

Customer reactions can be as variable as the number of customers served. Identify your team members based on their ability to be flexible. The customer must be treated uniquely and not as a number in a spreadsheet.

### Caring

Verbal and body language cues are very evident to customers and they will read between the lines. If your staff doesn't appear to care, then the customer will assume the company doesn't care either.

### Communication

Seek out people who can effectively convey your message to the target audience.

### Sincere Smile

You want to be around happy people. Your customers do too!

### Slow to Anger

Even with the most difficult and demanding customers, you need to never let them see you sweat. Being patient, kind and unwilling to lose control will go a long way in turning the tide on a negative situation. Your team should be able to take a break after a tough experience and you should reward the hard work and effort that goes into keeping their cool. Give them a chance to take a deep breath before taking on the next challenging customer.

*You Will Need to Develop Your Team and Provide Them with Sufficient Resources...*

### Training and Appropriate Tools

External resources are available (much more on this in Chapter Seven)

## Practice Makes Perfect

Allow new employees to observe you and other experienced employees with customers so they can see how it is done properly. Mock experience training is very helpful also.

## Inspect What You Expect

Don't leave the actual experience to chance. Observe, monitor and encourage staff to meet the daily challenges that come with the territory of customer interactions.

## Trickle Down Service

The tone and example that managers or senior leaders project will affect experience delivery.

## Employee Empowerment

Employees should be given latitude to make basic exceptions for customer preference.

Steve:

""I enjoy choosing my table at a restaurant and take offense when the hostess does not ask if the placement is satisfactory."

"I have always enjoyed Next Level captivating experiences at Ken Stewart's restaurants in Akron, Ohio, and a recent Friday evening date with my wife of 28 years, Robin, was no exception. I called to make a reservation a few days ahead for one of our favorite booths nestled in a private alcove, set apart from the main dining room with pulled back draperies. The friendly hostess answered my call promptly. When I asked for a booth, she offered to make a note but explained she couldn't guarantee the exact location."

"As we were driving to the restaurant that evening, I again called to see if 'our booth' would be available when we arrived 15 minutes later. The friendly hostess answered and said it looked like the booth was open but again could not guarantee the location. So, for the next 15 minutes I was thinking about 'our booth' and how I needed to hurry to arrive so not to miss out."

"Guess what? When we walked in, we were greeted as special guests and escorted to the exact booth we had requested. The service, food and entire experience for the rest of the evening was indeed captivating. So I should rate this as 100 percent, right? Well almost, but I still remember being anxious as we were driving. The experience would have been perfect had the hostess simply offered to reserve 'our booth' and put me at ease on the phone given that we called and were only a few minutes away.""

Let your people make appropriate exceptions to procedures when customers are asking for a favor that can easily be granted. This will help build loyalty both with the employee and the customer.

Allow employees to provide something special back to the customer if they express any feedback of dissatisfaction as part of their experience. A small token such as a free dessert or discount for future service will make a lasting impression and often dissolve lingering doubts about your company.

## The Buck Stops Here

Allow employees to escalate issues when needed directly to you or another appropriate high-level decision maker when they are unable to smooth over a situation personally. A supervisor who is really just the employee's peer with some seniority saying the same thing to a customer will only exasperate them further. To resolve an escalated issue, send the customer directly to the owner, director, or senior manager who should make the situation right with the customer on the spot. After the issue is resolved, ask for feedback, listen carefully and correct your processes so the failure does not reoccur.

*Taking Your Customer Care™ to the Next Level*

Steve:

"My wife, Robin, works with Plexus, a company that provides excellent health and wellness products. She placed a large phone order recently to share with a number of people she'd been communicating with. Apparently the person she talked to made an error and the package was never sent. She called back to check on the situation from her mobile phone and as she was explaining the issue, the line disconnected. This happened twice due to mobile connectivity issues as she was driving. The company escalated the issue directly to the senior vice president of customer care. He left her several voice messages and an email letting her know how sorry he was and that he was taking care of the issue immediately. She indeed received the products in the mail the following day. He had sent everything to her via overnight delivery at no additional charge to her. He modeled perfectly the philosophy of *Taking Your Customer Care™ to the Next Level.*"

Reward, Recognize and Request a Response

Thank and recognize your employees constantly. Never take them for granted. They are longing for your approval each and every day.

- Tell them you are going to recognize them.
- Recognize them with rewards.
- Then ask them for feedback on how they feel about their work and the way they are treated.

Pay It Forward

Customers cannot be taken for granted either. Establish a process to give back to your customers with gifts and thank you services. Shower them with appreciation for doing business with you. Embrace the concept of random acts of kindness.

Treat your Employees Care-fully and they will in turn treat your Customers Care-fully and Create *Next Level Customer Experiences.*

## Chapter Six

# DON'T LEAD FROM BEHIND: LEADERSHIP EMPOWERS YOUR TEAM TO DELIVER NEXT LEVEL CUSTOMER CARE™

*Lead by example...*
*Walk the walk...*
*Say what you mean and mean what you say...*

We have heard the slogans for the importance of strong leadership. And, YES, it does matter more than ever before as there is a leadership vacuum in many businesses today. Employees are dazed and confused with minimal support and lack of positive reinforcement. Front line staff feel their bosses don't care or understand how hard they work.

Society has encouraged an "us vs. them" mentality, which leads to resentment of income level disparity. When people know you care about them as individuals and have opportunity to interact with leaders through open communication there is a greater depth of respect. An environment that celebrates individual and group success and creates opportunity for advancement will cause people to thrive.

If you advertise that your company treats customers well, then you must deliver a great customer experience. And great experiences are delivered by great employees.

Observe how customers are experiencing your brand and how employees interact.

**Undercover Boss**

A Boston Market worker who ranted about his hatred of customers was fired after his colleague turned out to be an undercover top-level company executive. The man, named only as Ronnie, is the first person to get the boot from his firm during filming for the CBS reality show 'Undercover Boss.' "I literally hate customers more than anything in the entire world. I hate them so much. They're terrible. It's all about them all the time and they demand everything," Ronnie says.

But, unbeknown to him, his co-worker was not fictional trainee waitress Rachel Rand, but in fact the firm's Chief Brand Officer Sara Bittorf. The program shows her becoming livid with shift supervisor Ronnie, at times having to excuse herself from the kitchen so she can catch her breath. "My job's on the line. Here I am a representative of this brand and this is what happens. It can't happen on my watch," she is seen saying. "I can't have someone who just told me that they hate customers more than anything in the world serving our guests. That's the complete antithesis of what we stand for."

Deciding to tell Ronnie the truth of who she is, she then scolded him, before telling the branch manager and advising that Ronnie be fired. But Ronnie remained unrepentant, saying, "I would tell them my attitude would change but I didn't think it was that terrible. It's not wrong of me to hate people."

**The Philosophy of Leadership**

"Do not follow where the path may lead. Go instead where there is no path and leave a trail." – Ralph Waldo Emerson

"The single biggest way to impact an organization is to focus on leadership development. There is almost no limit to the potential of an organization that recruits good people, raises them up as leaders and continually develops them." – John Maxwell

"The true mark of a leader is the willingness to stick with a bold course of action — an unconventional business strategy, a unique product-development roadmap, a controversial marketing campaign — even as the rest of the world wonders why you're not marching in step with the status quo. In other words, real leaders are happy to zig while others zag. They understand that in an era of hyper-competition and non-stop disruption, the only way to stand out from the crowd is to stand for something special." – Bill Taylor, from the article, *Do You Pass the Leadership Test?*

**Customer Care™ Champion: Southwest Airlines**

Southwest Leads through Differentiation:

- It makes the customer experience as fun as possible.
- It "Goes the Extra Mile" for the customer.
- Its seat selection and boarding process is simpler and more straightforward than other airlines.
- It doesn't nickel and dime customers. (Other airlines charge extra for checked bags and for what they consider premium seats.)
- It isn't super serious. Staff members actually tell jokes and take calculated brand risks.

Average to poor customer service is the norm today. By emphasizing the customer experience, you will immediately differentiate your products and services

**Investing in Customer-Centric Strategies Improves ROI**

The key ingredient to experiencing higher ROI and profitability is to build an entirely customer-centric strategy. Low-cost European airline Ryanair cut its fees and restrictions, and loosened its policies to allow customers to bring more carry-on bags. The moves contributed to a 28 percent increase in passenger numbers from the previous year. This clearly illustrates that Customer Care™ and return on investment go hand in hand. Formulating and executing on a customer-centric strategy requires caring for your customers, hiring and training the right people, making the right connections, and maintaining perspective in changing conditions.

## Straighten Up and Hire Right

When new hires fail, 89 percent of the time it is for attitude. But how do you assess attitude?

Mark Murphy, founder of *Leadership IQ*, who studied more than 1000 companies while writing *Hiring for Attitude*, said in an article for Forbes.com, "Employee referrals work because who better to recruit stars with great attitudes than your current stars with great attitudes? Your current high performers probably had previous jobs where they worked with dozens, if not hundreds, of others. Based on those up-close-and-personal past interactions, they can assess how a potential candidate thinks, feels, reacts, produces and more. Attitudinal factors that are important to know when assessing whether a potential candidate will fit, or fail, in your company."

Murphy interviewed Stacy Green, senior vice president of human resources at A+E Networks, where the entire extended management team is recruited through networking and personal relationships. She said: "I can't recommend someone I met in an hour interview who was recommended by a recruiter. I want a relationship with every person hired. A+E's referral rate is so high that we do very little external recruiting anymore."

Murphy recommends: "Identify your uniqueness, raise the volume on your employee-referred applicants, start actively networking, and develop a pipeline of talent that you might not hire for another year. And of course, all the while remember that the reason you're doing this is to recruit stars that have the right attitudes to fit your culture."

## Keep Promises to Employees and They Will Keep Promises to Customers

The No. 1 most important reason that employees state as the reason for being loyal to a company is their belief and confidence in their senior leaders.

The No. 2 factor driving employee loyalty is growth and development. Education is especially important to Millennials and your best performing team members. Provide staff with resources to gain valuable skills to advance in their careers. Consider on-site soft skills training, technical training and certifications.

**"Under-promise and Over-deliver to Your Employees...Teach them by Example to Over-deliver on Promises to Customers!"**

## Identify Where Employees Fit-Best in Your Organization

Tim Roche of Right Management says: "Our research suggests that nearly half the employees in any given company are in the wrong functional roles – jobs they aren't particularly suited for or productive at ... jobs that accommodate their weaknesses rather than harness their strengths ... jobs they tolerate but find little satisfaction performing."

Roche explains: "Most organizations have not developed the 'people systems' capable of identifying talent in the wrong space and transitioning them into the right roles doing the right work. As a result, employee engagement and productivity suffer, driving organizational performance down. Imagine the impact if you could reposition people across the organization into roles that are better aligned to their occupational interests and strengths. If you could substantially increase the performance of even 25 percent of your workforce – let alone 50 percent — what would be the impact on your overall organizational performance?"

## Map Out a Career Path - Promote From Within

How many of your management staff started as front line team members? In an established business the number should be staggering. For new businesses, make this your goal. Document and share these stories inside and outside the company. Celebrate dedication and commitment each and every day.

## ***Communication!!!***

## So, Are You Ready to *Take your Customer Care*™ *to the Next Level*?

### Be Engaged Yourself

Modern Survey reports that 33 percent of leaders at organizations with 100 or more employees are currently looking for a job at another organization. As CEO Don MacPherson says: "That's one-third of all your leaders actively looking to leave! To provide some context, just two years ago – when Modern Survey began collecting data on the item 'I am currently looking for a job at another organization' – only 22 percent of leaders agreed. The percentage of leaders looking has steadily climbed since spring 2013."

### Be an Influencer

The ability to influence positive and lasting change in others is essential to success in business today. Be a change agent yourself by communicating what it will take and be open to your team members' needs and questions. Change will come when the people in your organization take action to do things differently and it starts with you!

Be Relational

How to develop a better relationship with every member of your team:

- Recognize excellence...Praise individuals publicly and criticize privately
- Identify growth areas...Nip issues in the bud. Do not accept subpar performance.
- Motivate with new opportunities for greater responsibility. People generally want to be promoted and grow with a company. Provide incentives to showcase individual strengths by adding more challenging tasks.
- Honesty and trust. Be real and let your people be real back to you. Open communication will help you know what is going on.

**Don't surround yourself with "YES" people; rather develop "MAKE IT HAPPEN" people.**

If the process isn't working, employees will not insulate your customers from the heat.

- NO, not NEVER...When you have to shoot down an employee proposal, be sure to listen completely as to why he or she is suggesting the idea. There is likely something you need to do differently. Explain why not and then work with them on a solution to the issue even if their initially suggested alternative won't work for the business.
- Listen to the Pulse of your Organization. Conduct interviews with current employees. Open the door to conversation regarding retention, growth, career opportunity and individual employee goals.

## Create a Performance Improvement Plan (PIP)

Every HR leader knows it is critical to clearly document the areas where low performers are missing the mark and list out specific action plans for expected improvements through a Performance Improvement Plan (PIP). That same approach can be tailored to the organization as a whole. Call it your Customer Care™ PIP.

Customer Experience Begins and Ends with your People

How do they react? What are their attitudes? What will we do to reset expectations? How can our people benefit from these changes? Sell the benefits.

Listen to Customers

They will tell you what should be done differently. Be open to change!

Customer Care™ Relies on Systems, Policies and Procedures

These tools provide the framework of your process and must be integrated throughout your operations. Change must be carefully planned to understand the impact across all areas of the business to prevent unintended setbacks.

## Be All You Can Be

Based on working for a number of outstanding managers over the years (and some who were not) we have developed a list of the dozen qualities that distinguish truly great leaders from those who are poor, marginal or just plain OK:

1. Caring how others feel and helping them accomplish their goals.
2. Welcoming people to speak freely, listening and being open to criticism.
3. Keeping a positive attitude and perspective.

4. Coaching to develop the right behaviors in others.
5. Influencing a culture of creativity and thinking outside the box.
6. Showering praise to the team and not assuming all the credit personally for success.
7. Becoming a lifelong student in a continual quest for knowledge to be the best you can be.
8. Setting a bold vision for the future, inspiring others to join in the search to make the dreams a reality.
9. Learning from failure by getting back up to fight another day with effervescent energy.
10. Realizing you are human, make mistakes, own them and take action to change for the better.
11. Championing the ethical approach in every decision and speaking up for what is right.
12. Maintaining composure...Never let them see you sweat.

**People Follow True Leaders**

We must be dedicated to make the improvements needed, and the staff will be also. Move forward and never look back. Lead your team to deliver *Next Level Customer Care*™, which will result in Customer Retention.

## Chapter Seven

# TEACH EMPLOYEES TO CARE... TRAIN, TRAIN AND RETRAIN: THE CUSTOMER IS ALWAYS RIGHT

Employees must be trained to treat customers with the utmost respect.

Steve:

"I heard a story once about a customer of a large grocery store. He asked an employee at the bakery counter a few questions about the cinnamon rolls being offered for customers to sample. The employee told him that the pastries were very fattening and he should consider losing some weight!"

**Teach Them HOW to Do the Job with CARE**

In today's sophisticated business world, no one can get anywhere without appropriate training. And with more advanced or technical interactions, more intense training is required.

Nadji:

"My daughter and son-in-law recently opened a new retail concept in the largest shopping mall in Las Vegas, Art Montage, where they sell a variety of unique, multi-dimensional artwork. The software designed to manage their customer purchase transactions required personalized training. I was impressed with the excellent Customer Care™ provided to them from the software company representatives. The computer implementation engineer spent two full training days in a row onsite with them and their staff, ensuring everyone on the team was fully versed in all aspects of the system integration. And then again the following day, the engineer called just to check if they had any questions or experienced any issues after he had returned home."

**Training expenses are often one of the first areas to be reduced in corporate America when trying to boost the bottom line.**

**We believe the reason is that training is viewed as an expense when it should be viewed as an investment in customer loyalty.**

Reducing employee training to improve profitability will only lead to further alienating customers as front line staff are even less prepared to handle their needs. In addition, employees will continue to view the company as uninterested in personal growth and although they may punch the clock, it is likely they are not really 'showing up' for your business' or the customer's best interests.

According to a 2012 study from the Society for Human Resources Management, 36 percent of employees surveyed said that professional development and job-specific training were "very important" to their job satisfaction, and only about half were satisfied with it. Helping employees build skills and knowledge not only ensures a highly efficient workforce, but also bolsters confidence and engagement.

A great way to enhance your training expertise is to learn from the companies doing things well and adapt your own policies appropriately.

## Apple's Five Steps of Service

Gizmodo Senior Staff Writer, Sam Biddle shared Apple's training process in the article, *How To Be a Genius: This is Apple's Secret Employee Training Manual*. Biddle commented: "We read Apple's secret Genius training manual from cover to cover. It's a penetrating look inside Apple: psychological mastery, banned words, roleplaying—you've never seen anything like it."

According to Gizmodo, the Apple in-store customer experience is summed up with an acrostic based on the five letters in the word Apple. The five words correspond to five specific steps that employees are trained to walk through with customers.

**A:** Approach customers with a personalized, warm welcome.
**P:** Probe politely to understand the customer's needs (ask open-ended questions).
**P:** Present a solution for the customer to take home today.
**L:** Listen for and resolve any issues or concerns.
**E:** End with a fond farewell and an invitation to return.

By the last step the customer should feel welcomed, empowered, happy, and eager to return.

## Technology Advances JetBlue Passenger Care

"When you think of good customer service, Amazon and Zappos may come to mind, but a major commercial airline may not. JetBlue is working to change that perception by incorporating new technologies that focus on improving customer service," reports Lauren Brousell, senior writer for CIO magazine.

JetBlue's CIO, Eash Sundaram has led the development of a customer-facing technology transformation. He says JetBlue needed to be about customer service and technology as much as it was about getting passengers to their destinations. "We think of ourselves as a customer service company that happens to fly planes," says Sundaram. "So when you think of the customer service aspect of JetBlue, it's all about personalization and how we take care of customer needs. Technology plays such an integral role in addressing our customer needs."

For example, after the roll-out of free in-flight Wi-Fi, JetBlue provided iPads to flight attendants and crew members to deliver more targeted customer service. Using the Inflight Service Assistant app, flight attendants can view a seat map, click on a customer and know if he or she is a Mosaic loyalty member, or if it's his or her birthday. Flight attendants can also see if a passenger has a connecting flight and in the case of a delay, can suggest other flight options.

Enable your team to customize experiences through the use of intelligent technologies, and as a result they will be empowered to strengthen customer relationships.

**Apply Customer Care™ Disciplines**

Harley Manning, vice president of Forrester Research was quoted by Jim Tierney of Loyalty 360 as saying: "In Forrester's annual Customer Experience Index of more than 150 brands, only 8 percent received 'excellent' grades."

Corporate training curriculum should incorporate an understanding of the six customer experience disciplines that Forrester has outlined.

Strategy

The corporate strategy must be specific, clear, and memorable.

Customer Understanding

A brand's ability to understand and identify customer expectations is crucial in supplying a great customer experience. Create a consistent shared understanding of who customers are, what they want and need, and how they perceive the interactions they're having with the company.

### Design

The customer experience has to be purposely designed and tested to envision and implement customer interactions that meet and exceed customer needs. It spans the complex systems of people, products, interfaces, services, and spaces that customers encounter in retail locations, over the phone, or through digital media like websites and mobile apps.

### Measurement

Capture all customer touch points and then focus exclusively on what really matters to customers.

### Governance

**Holding people accountable for their roles in the customer experience ecosystem helps prevent bad experiences. Make it part of Employee Job Descriptions and Evaluations.**

### Culture

Culture demonstrates the power of empathy, comprising practices that create a system of shared values and behaviors focusing employees on habits that deliver great Customer Care™.

Employees need help to connect the dots between the expected customer experience and their routine duties. Your training should spell out what the experience should look and sound like to make customers feel their expectations were exceeded and the process was simple and enjoyable for them.

## Words are Powerful

Of course you won't allow employees to use slang or crude language, but teach your team to focus on everyday language for opportunities to make an impression.

Authentic

Do your words sound like a personal connection, or are they "corporate speak"?

Positive

Are you focusing on the interaction, even when it's an uncomfortable discussion?

Memorable

Can you capture a customer's attention with a particularly clever, funny or meaningful phrase?

Keep the conversations with your customers interesting and friendly. Surprise them with the care and interest you take in them as individuals.

## Go Fish

The FISH! Philosophy was inspired by a business that is world famous for its incredible energy and commitment to service—the Pike Place Fish Market in Seattle. They have identified four simple practices that help anyone bring new energy and commitment to their work.

Organizations around the world are using the FISH! Philosophy to:

- **Provide amazing care so customers will want to come back again and again**
- **Build a culture where employees love to give their best every day**
- **Build effective leaders who inspire through their example**
- **Improve teamwork and build trust**

Customers go through their same routine day in and day out. When they reach your business, whether it is in person, over the phone, or even in writing, you are just one stop in their day. Starbucks teaches its team members the importance of making emotional connections with customers. Once that connection is made, you increase your base of loyal customers, and reach a whole new network through those loyal customers.

**Develop Empathy among Team Members**

Here are a few tips for developing empathy in adults:

Spend Time with People who are Different than You

Encourage opportunities to do this by setting up cross-functional work groups with staff from various departments.

Think Like the Customer

Immerse your team members to experience the feelings of customers in their interactions with the brand to better understand the way they think and feel.

Acting Lessons and Role Play

Acting is at its core, stepping into someone else's shoes. Identify ways to nudge your employees outside their comfort zones in training, so they are able to react appropriately with unique personalities in the real world workplace.

## **The Art of Listening:**

**Effective listening is perhaps the most valuable skill you can teach your employees. It is absolutely necessary to determine and deliver what the customer needs and wants. Listening enables you to draw customers into an interactive conversation in which they can ask perceptive questions, probe for reactions, and respond to those reactions appropriately.**

Most people are not natural listeners, nor are they trained in the art of listening. Most of us either don't hear the message at all, or hear it but misinterpret its meaning.

Listening can be especially, and understandably, difficult in situations when your staff members are under time pressure to handle tasks, and are concentrating on what they have to say or do next instead of paying close attention to what the customer is actually communicating.

We have found people generally struggle to be present in conversations. In conversations with customers, it is critical to be able to pivot when the discussion suddenly changes course. Encourage your staff to repeat back the context of what they are hearing to the other person. This is especially important in phone call interactions.

**Here are specific techniques you can teach employees to use that will demonstrate real interest in the customer--an excellent way to establish rapport and a powerful form of communication.**

- **Tune out distractions and focus on each customer as if he or she is the most important interaction of the day.**
- **Concentrate on what the customer is saying rather than thinking about what YOU want to say.**
- **Don't interrupt; a customer's willingness to talk, within a reasonable time period, represents a golden opportunity to find out the problem/situation.**
- **Don't jump to conclusions.**
- **Be aware of voice tone and inflection, which are as important as the words being said.**
- **Occasionally repeat what the customer has said--it shows attention and comprehension.**
- **Ask for clarification if something isn't understood.**
- **Smile sincerely.**
- **Control emotions and be kind, no matter how rude the customer might be.**

Teaching by example is, of course, a great way to make a point. Leaders who listen to employee needs and encourage listening in staff meetings will help reinforce the value of this important skill.

Nadji:

""One of my favorite supermarkets where we live in Connecticut is Stew Leonard's Farm Fresh Foods. Its website proclaims it features, 'fresh milk products and great customer service!'"

"The Stew Leonard's history can be traced back to the early 1920s, to Clover Farms Dairy, run by Stew's father Charles in Norwalk, Conn. It was a state of the art dairy by the standards of the time - with a pasteurizing and bottling plant, and fresh milk delivered daily. Stew's dream was to build a retail dairy store where children could watch milk being bottled, while mothers did their shopping in a farmer's market atmosphere. In December 1969, Stew Leonard's opened its doors - a 17,000-square-foot store carrying just eight items. The store has expanded to become the World's

Largest Dairy Store, and now operates four renowned grocery stores, with annual sales of almost $400 million and almost 2,000 team members."

"My experience with the store and employees has always been extraordinary, and my family continues to return week after week. At the entrance to the store, there is a large rock, emblazoned with the following mantra:

**#1 Rule: The Customer Is Always Right.**
**#2 Rule: If You Think the Customer is not Right, Please Refer to Rule # 1."**

"Clearly Stew Leonard understood the key to *Taking Your Customer Care™ to the Next Level*, and his legacy lives on.""

Providing good training and thorough preparation on how to provide excellent Customer Care™ will give employees confidence to be themselves in their communications, recognizing the ultimate goal is to, *Go the Extra Mile for your Customer.*

Chapter Eight

# LISTEN AND LEARN: GAIN A COMPLETE VIEW OF YOUR CUSTOMERS

Put your customers under the microscope and analyze their needs. David Cooperstein, formerly at Forrester Research believes businesses should move past being customer-centric or customer-focused into being customer-obsessed.

Great customer engagement won't happen if there is only focus on making the sale. Engagement is all about nurturing the relationships between you and your customers. Your success will be largely dependent on your company's ability to offer ways to become connected in a meaningful way throughout the customer journey and beyond.

"We're in a world of servant selling, where the best way to persuade, the best way to influence, the best way to sell is to serve first and sell next." Daniel Pink, *A Whole New Mind.*

**What is your Brand Voice?**

Are you consistent in your communications and interactions with your customers?

Create experiences that become stories your customers will share about the way they were treated when doing business with your company.

*Nadji Tehrani; Steve Brubaker*

## A Moment to Remember

A moment happens at a specific place and time. No two moments are exactly alike. Think of your own personal stories, from a first kiss to a moment of triumph. What happened? Who was there? What did they say? What would we have seen?

Now think about this in terms of your brand. Every brand lives for customers as a series of touch points. If you can put your customers at that moment where they feel what it's like to encounter the best value of your brand, you're one moment closer to connecting them to your brand.

Skype: "Stay Together"

Skype's "Stay Together" campaign demonstrates how people are using technology to develop deep, emotional relationships across great distances. It was a shift from talking about its product and features to talking about the emotional benefits of using its product. In 2013 it featured two young girls, Sarah from Indiana and Paige from New Zealand. Both girls who were born without a full left arm connected through Skype, learning from one another's experiences. They were able to teach each other valuable lessons about self-confidence, and share those iconic teenage-girl moments, like swapping hair and makeup tips. The two girls didn't just keep in touch—Skype allowed them to become best friends, even while living on separate continents. In the ad they meet for the very first time after communicating for eight years from across the globe. The campaign is global and spans multiple channels, but it's also personal and emotional. It connects with the audience.

New York Life: "Keep Good Going"

Fortune 100 company, New York Life was founded in 1845 and is the largest mutual life insurance company in the United States. Its television, print, digital and outdoor campaign carries the theme

"Keep Good Going," which is meant to extol the virtues of buying life insurance and other financial products.

"At New York Life, we believe in perpetuating the good that is all around us. Keep Good Going describes both our purpose as a business and our relationship with our customers, today, tomorrow, and over the long term. The stories and videos our customer share have touched and inspired us to celebrate the ways we all Keep Good Going every day.

The company has connected personally with customers. It has mastered the art of delivering on its powerful, emotional promise.

Saks Fifth Avenue:

Saks Fifth Avenue has developed a strategy to leverage customer lifecycle programs. It works to deliver the right message at the right time to customers. Saks Fifth Avenue uses data specifically to effectively deliver:

- Real-time welcome campaigns
- Waitlist/back in stock programs
- Re-engagement strategies

Best Buy:

Best Buy audited customer experiences before, during, and after purchase. It realized that it focused primarily on the customer experience before and during purchase and forgot about shaping the experience afterward. It then worked on creating an "after" experience to encourage customers to return.

**Teach every member of your organization to walk in the customers' shoes, understand their perspective first-hand and then deliver care in the way they would want to experience it.**

Nonprofit organizations should analyze when donors tend to lapse (no gift has been given for a period of time) and implement a pre-lapsing strategy. Start communicating differently to prevent donors from lapsing and hopefully re-cement their loyalty.

In every way, shape and form that your business comes into contact with prospects, customers and friends of friends of both; you are performing a marketing function. So let me ask you this: Have you considered the impact or lack of impact of every touch point in your customer's journey?

**Customer Journey Map**

Design the flows of who, what, when, how and why we connect with customers. How much do you really know about your customers besides their names, phone numbers and addresses?

In today's highly-competitive marketplace, it's important to understand why customers make the decisions they do, how they feel about those choices and what type of experience they had. Armed with this information, you can start delivering a better customer experience. In order to do so, however, you have to gather the right data.

Customer analytics, or data gathered about customer behavior which is often used to make key business decisions, is hugely beneficial for contact centers as it gives them insight into the mind and motivation of the customer.

Adam Toporek, in the book, *Be Your Customer's Hero: Real-World Tips & Techniques for the Service Front Lines* helps to clarify: "While the mere exercise of mapping your customer's journey has value, the ultimate goal is to improve your customer's experience by understanding what they go through at each touch point and improving the quality of that experience."

"Using the 80/20 approach, start with your most important touch points, and ask the questions: How can I make this quicker and easier? Can I remove parts of the process to make it go quicker?

Can I empower employees to make the process easier by solving more issues in real time?"

Gathering customer data can help identify and measure important trends as well as see what topics are trending, such as recurring complaints or inquiries. Once you've identified these trends you can then make strategic decisions to get ahead and improve the customer experience – whether it's revamping a product based on customers' reactions or improving the overall sales process.

**The bottom line is this: Customer feedback is worth its weight in gold as it will help you reinvent and improve customer experience, while simultaneously strengthening customer loyalty and improving your bottom line.**

And it's important that brands do not shy away from identifying both the good and bad sentiments customers may be harboring. Learning from a specific customer's negative experience is essential to making the necessary changes to improve the experience for everyone.

Technology gives customers new decision-making and purchasing power. Potential buyers can access information about products, services, pricing, and brand reputation from anywhere, anytime. Because of this, you must know and understand your customers by leveraging customer data to identify market segments and target your communications appropriately.

Sanjay Dholakia, CMO at Marketo, developed a simple framework to use when engaging with consumers. He suggests marketers engage customers by A, B, C, D and E:

- A. As individuals
- B. Based on behavior
- C. Continuously over time
- D. Directed towards an outcome
- E. Everywhere they are

**Tech Touch Points**

<u>Enable Multi-Channel Engagement through Strategic Technological Implementation</u>

To create a personalized experience, the self-service options must provide the ability to seamlessly connect with live communication upon demand. Customer data and the trail of support detail should flow throughout the interaction with Customer Relationship Management or more appropriately called *Customer Engagement Management* systems. Customers should never have to repeat steps with you such as entering their name, account detail, security information, etc., when they want to seamlessly transfer from self-service to live support.

The goal is to predict, when possible the needs of customers and any problems before they even speak to an employee. Predictive analytics enables a more efficient and accurate handling of customer interactions, delivering a huge boost to satisfaction.

Companies should engage with customers in three ways: through assisted service, self-service, and connected service. Assisted service includes channels where customers engage with a person. Self-service includes channels where customers engage with technology, such as IVR or the corporate website. And connected service begins with customers trying to resolve their issues in a self-service channel such as a mobile app. If they are unable to complete the interaction using self-service, they are seamlessly transferred to assisted service, such as an agent in a contact center.

**Recency and Frequency**

Keeping customers active in their journey with you is important. Identify the stages of engagement and put a process in place to encourage continued movement in your direction.

## The First Purchase or Inquiry is a Critical First Step in the Relationship

A critical first step is that first connection, but then the hard work of engagement begins. Continuing a relationship takes far more effort than asking for and getting a first date. Being attentive, communicating, following-up and being instantly available when you get a call back will move you toward a second purchase. Find out if the people are using the product, if they have questions, is there any additional special service or assistance you may provide to make their experience with your company captivating?

When buying a new car, the salesperson provides education on the many features and benefits. When you drive home, there are buttons, lights and sensors that require action. The dealership should have a knowledgeable and patient team member walk you through the settings. And provide follow-up to help months or years later when you inevitably forget how to move the clock forward one hour as daylight savings time begins, or reconfigure your Bluetooth connection to add a new device. How simple was the experience for customers to connect with you and get the help needed? Will they remember your service attitude when they aren't writing a check? Will the experience be as delighting as it was when they first purchased the $60,000 vehicle?

Steve:

""A friend of mine recently bought a new vehicle. He was able to preselect his custom choices online. Each option came with a specific communicated price tag, so he was educated on his exact needs before ever approaching the dealership. The salesperson found nearly the exact car he wanted and treated him like royalty."

"Once the sale was consummated though, he waited 45 minutes before the finance office was open for him to sign the final paperwork. There was little communication as to why he was waiting in the general lobby for so long."

"Imagine if the salesperson had escorted him directly without delay to the finance office? Or, if that wasn't possible due to so many purchases at the same moment, why not take the customer to a New Customer VIP Lounge, where he is offered a glass of wine and specialty refreshments reserved for premier customers?"

"Although my friend is happy with his vehicle, the experience could have been better. The car dealer could have created an experience that *Took Customer Care™ to the Next Level.* That first impression would then be communicated numerous times to others and would become a differentiator for the business, separating it from competitors.""

Tell your customers something they don't already know about your company, products or services. Continued communication with your audience with helpful information will help to propel the relationship forward.

## You Don't Bring Me Flowers Anymore

We have all experienced relationships that have reached the proverbial sunset. Develop communications to remind customers you are always available to serve them. Alert them to an expiring special offer. Share a new design or feature you are offering. Ask again for their business and provide an incentive to rekindle the flame. Be sure the message is highly targeted, personalized based on their situation, and include a strong call to action as if it were your last ditch effort to re-engage.

### What Do You Do When the Customer Relationship Goes South?

Tracey Schelmetic, TMCnet contributor asked readers that question.

She shared: "We're all familiar with the blind spots in our cars: those points just beyond the edges of our bumpers where our vision stops and the potential for deadly collisions starts. In business, there are blind spots as well...they may not put anyone in danger of mortal injury, but they can be destructive all the same. Often, they have to do with customer relationships and the lack of visibility many companies have into previous interactions."

Schelmetic goes on to say: "To most [companies] today, customers aren't customers, they are a series of communications that request something: a solution to a problem, an answer to a question, or remedial action on a mistake. This is the wrong approach: a customer is a human being whose relationship with a company should be one holistic experience, and everyone who has contact with customers should have this information instantly and readily available. By approaching customers as simply transaction numbers or trouble tickets, companies run the risk of driving loyal customers away and failing to capture potential new lifelong customers."

"The following scenario," she continues, "is probably familiar to most people: you receive an erroneous bill from a company (perhaps a double bill or a bill for a service you don't receive). You call the company and it takes eons to straighten out. Perhaps you have taken the time to scan a cancelled check or an invoice in order to prove that you are right. The company promises to fix the problem, but the following month, you receive the same erroneous bill. There are two ways the next phone call could go:

- Scenario A: When the customer calls, the agent takes a moment to glance over any previous interactions. Armed with the knowledge of why the customer is calling, the agent can apologize profusely – and be forgiving of the customer's understandably huffy tone -- and promise that the matter will be handled, and follow through. In this scenario, the relationship will probably be saved.

- Scenario B: The agent picks up the call blind, listens to the customer's problem and writes him or her off as a complainer. The customer must then explain and prove the error all over again, and the agent takes offense at the customer's aggravated tone, perhaps even suggesting that the customer 'calm down.' In this scenario, the customer hangs up the phone, screams, and informs all of his or her friends to avoid the company."

"Customer consultant Micah Solomon, writing for Forbes, says what separates good customer service providers from bad is the quality of the customer relationship recovery process, or having a backup plan when things go wrong. 'It's crucial that you have a world-class customer service recovery process in place for when things go south,' Solomon wrote. 'It doesn't work to wing it every time a customer is irritated, frustrated, or flat-out furious. No matter how superb your product or service is, every company needs a service recovery process with the goal of restoring (or even enhancing) customer satisfaction, as well as reducing the possibility of a recurrence.'"

Schelmetic concludes: "For starters, prevention of blind spots is critical: if your people at their desktop do not have easy and fast access to overviews of the customer relationship, you are doomed to be a Scenario B company. While you may not be able to knock the ball out of the park every time, if you have a backup plan specifically designed to save the customer relationship, you'll ensure you're not actively driving customers away."

What Would Your Best Customer Do?

Capture the data of which customers react to certain messages in specific ways. Track the metrics and then identify groups of similar customers. Pattern your process to help predict the next actions of the various groups.

Your best customers may not only be the ones who spend the most. Look at your strongest influencers for word of mouth impact, online and on the street.

**Not all Customers are Created Equal**

We need to strategically engage customers based on their behaviors, tendencies, and interests. Companies can move on from "one size fits all" approaches and tailor the experience to the consumer based on their preferred activity and channel—whether that be blogging, social media, email marketing, etc.

Steve:

""Restaurants ask for feedback quite often and include information on the receipt with the details of how to respond. They usually offer a future discount as a way to thank customers for taking time out to share input. Most of the time there is only an online website option. I prefer to call and give feedback and will not go online to do the survey. It is just my preference. I'm sure some people prefer to enter the survey information online."

"Why not offer both options? Online and Telephone Channels""

Make it EASY and convenient for customers to interact with your company, whether to give feedback or contact you for any reason. Provide customers the flexibility to choose the channel they prefer most.

**Customers Perceive Advantages from their Unique Perspective**

Location, Location, Location

Prime locations for shopping centers change as population and demographics evolve throughout communities. What is old is new again. Lifestyle centers are expanding across the country mimicking the vibrant downtowns of yesteryear. Maintaining visibility and customer connection is more complex as brands move their points of presence to ever-changing locales.

## Place and Time

Customers want choice in how they communicate with you: face to face, web, text, 24/7 phone support. Bank branches are now located in most supermarkets with extended hours of service.

## Social

Online communities are contagious, similarly to social clubs of the past. Bars, department stores, homes, and churches were the main social gathering venues during the 60's, 70's, 80's and 90's. Today, coffee shops, mobile devices, and online connections have become even more popular for engaging social interactions.

## Multi-Channel

It is essential to provide and capture all points of interaction to offer the complete package of *Next Level Customer Care*™.

Examine every area of the customer experience to deliver a multi-sensory approach. Develop a matrix of the five senses and how customers experience your brand through all five.

The Golden Rule in reverse: Treat others the way they prefer to be treated. You do not determine customer preferences, they do. It is your job to identify and serve in the areas where customers are expecting you to be present.

## Different Strokes for...

Create targeted and unique messaging for key customer profiles.

## Baby Boomers

According to Nielsen, in less than five years, 50 percent of the U.S. population will be over the age of 50. They'll not only control 70 percent of the nation's disposable income, but they also stand to inherit $15 trillion in the next 20 years.

AARP sets a gold standard for brands that know how to market to those in their golden years. The AARP website has tailored its interface for older people new to the web, and has launched its TEK program (Technology, Education, Knowledge) with bold-colored, user-friendly tutorials, including lessons on how to use hashtags and even "Cyber proof Your Phone." Still, nowhere does AARP mention that its patrons are senior citizens or "old." Instead, it uses phrases such as "life re-imagined," "real possibilities," and "you've still got it."

## Millennials

Millennials are generally far more concerned about the environment and social causes than Baby Boomers. Creating images that will draw connection to positive social outcomes is more critical than ever before.

- <u>SeaWorld</u>: SeaWorld has struggled to counteract negative media attention and pressure from animal-rights groups over its treatment of killer whales following the 2013 documentary "Blackfish," which shed an unflattering light on the company's methods and was broadcast on CNN. Millennials grew up watching "Free Willy" and are generally concerned with the humane treatment of animals. Even though SeaWorld is well known as a leader in animal rescue care and conservation, the brand image has been tattered, and attendance is in free fall.

- <u>ALS Ice Bucket Challenge:</u> Millennials are actually one of the most active and vocal generations since their grandparents of the 60's and 70's. They're passionate and have the ability online to spread their message almost at the speed of light. Millennials were a big factor in the viral sensation of summer 2014's ALS Ice Bucket Challenge being so successful.

- *Dove and Coca-Cola:* Adweek reported that Dove and Coca-Cola were targeting better engagement with the much sought-after Millennial segment by attempting to make the audience feel "happier." According to a recent study by ZenithOptimedia, The Pursuit of Happiness, brands that can help Millennials achieve happiness stand the best chance of securing long-lasting and profitable relationships with that consumer group.

  Dove and Coca-Cola took their recent happiness-oriented campaigns to Twitter using targeted campaigns to turn online hate into something positive. With branded hashtags, the brands attempted to use marketing to make the Internet a happier, friendlier place. With #SpeakBeautiful, which will continue throughout the year, Dove hopes to foster positive self-esteem for women and girls. For Coke, #MakeItHappy used ASCII art—which generates images out of lines of text—to target different hateful tweets and turn those words into cheery imagery. According to Coke, its campaign received 95 percent positive and neutral social responses.

**New Boom**

NPR recently ran a series on Millennials called New Boom. It interviewed a handful of Millennials on their thoughts around marketing and brand relationships. Millennials have been quite clear about wanting brands to give them space to explore the products/brand experience on their own. They want brands to invite them to interact. Jacob Weiss, 28, said: "We don't want to be bombarded with advertisements or other bits of marketing in spaces that are personal to us." Another Millennial, Antonus Siler, 34, explained further: "If I could say anything to the advertisers, it'd be this: Entertain me, make me happy, capture my attention, speak to me and then leave me the heck alone."

## Multicultural Connections

Multicultural audiences are some of the most digitally-savvy consumers in the United States. They over-index on smartphone ownership and digital media streaming. They over-index for direct contact with authors, artists and brands through social media.

The US Hispanic population is the single-fastest growing population segment of young buyers in America. They live and breathe on digital media channels at rates more prominent than other ethnicities - they are not on the back burner of power and influence, they are the leaders of today's digital marketing revolution. Yet while the multicultural influence on digital channels is increasing rapidly, they're often a secondary component of a core marketing campaign.

Just as traditional marketing and digital marketing must be linked, so should multicultural marketing with core goals and strategy. To connect all of those components more clearly, digital marketing is multicultural marketing.

## Most Customer Experience Improvement Efforts Fail

Margaret Harrist of Oracle reported in Forbes: "The most well-intentioned customer experience improvement plans often go awry unless they're woven into a single holistic approach. These plans often start with people working diligently to improve their group's systems and processes, while forgetting that customers interact with the company—not the email team, social team, or support team. Piecemeal changes can end up providing an even more disjointed and frustrating experience for customers.

*Nadji Tehrani; Steve Brubaker*

They tend to become places where processes break down, where pieces don't connect, or where a company doesn't offer the right help, guidance, or options."

Listening to customers is essential to identifying and understanding their needs. Developing a care philosophy focused on customer needs will differentiate your brand as an industry leader.

## Chapter Nine

# THE PRINCIPLES FOR TAKING YOUR CUSTOMER CARE™ TO THE NEXT LEVEL

### Creating Customer Care™ Loyalty

What is your company culture saying to the customer? Should I stay or should I go? Are your customers repeating the rallying cry of Mick Jagger and The Rolling Stones, "I Can't Get No Satisfaction"?

Why do so many companies focus their efforts almost exclusively on acquiring new customers? Keeping customers happy is difficult, as they will move on to your competitor if they're subject to poor service. Thirty-seven percent of consumers say they will switch companies after a single poor customer service experience, according to the American Express 2014 Global Customer Service Barometer.

**Steve:**

"I become irritated when I notice advertised promotions offering significant discounts to new customers that I am not eligible for as a loyal customer. A number of years ago I received an ad in my mailbox offering a much lower price for cable service than I was currently paying from my provider. I called to take advantage of the savings but was told the deal was only for new customers. I asked what I needed to do to become a new customer again and was told that it would be necessary to disconnect service for six months and then reconnect again at that time to receive the lower price. Wouldn't it cost more to send a technician out and lose six months of revenue? Did they consider the risk of me choosing an alternate solution such as satellite?"

## **Customer Engagement and Employee Engagement Really Are Mutually Exclusive; You Cannot Have One Without the Other.**

Your employees create the environment and fulfill your customers' service expectations. Customers demand attention and quality. They provide feedback with their wallets opening up or their feet marching in the direction of your competition.

Steve:

""I receive email, promotions and invites daily for new products, conferences, training programs, etc. with the latest technology solutions promising to solve every business problem and create Utopia."

**"In 30 years I have not found one out of the box solution that does it all"**

"Many are helpful in meeting specific needs but not all inclusive.""

**There is No Silver Bullet**

It takes a clear and documented process, a relentless focus on the details and dedicated leadership to create excellence. Continually the process must be improved, listening for and acting on every sign of potential breakage or lapses in the delivery of your brand promise.

**Are you Relevant Today?**

Customers are hyper connected. They are also overloaded and suffer from what is being referred to as "content clutter

*Taking Your Customer Care™ to the Next Level*

shock." Studies show that each of us is bombarded with nearly 3000 messages a day. Customers are looking for more relevant connections and ever greater meaning in their lives. Simply put, the bar is now even higher for marketers to vault over.

Macy's is shopping for its next growth opportunity as U.S. department stores struggle to hold onto shoppers. Behind Macy's moves are the cold realities that its core industry is under siege: department stores' share of total U.S. general merchandise, apparel, accessories and furniture sales has been cut by more than half over the last two decades. Department stores' slice of that $1 trillion pie has gone from 33 percent in 1992 to 13.3 percent in 2014, according to U.S. Census data.

If Macy's does it right, analysts say the retailer could use a new off-price concept to court younger and thriftier Millennial customers – who might later become customers of the flagship Macy's brand.

Customers are placing greater and greater importance on the perception of the company offering services, sometimes more than the perception of the services themselves. This explains why companies are highly focused on the perception of their business relating to the environment, the economy, and most importantly the impact on their clients' unique experience.

**Community involvement**

Employees are motivated when they can care about something bigger than themselves. This is why it's important to clearly define your company mission. Giving back and encouraging every employee to make a difference by enabling them to volunteer is important. Follow your heart programs celebrate employees who give of their time and talents to the organizations and missions they feel are near and dear to their hearts. This is cultural. If the owners and managers are philanthropic and you recognize team members who generously give back, more and more of your staff will follow your lead.

**Steve:**

"As a lifelong employee of InfoCision over the past 30 years, I have admired the generosity of company founders, Gary and Karen Taylor. They have given of their personal resources to many local charitable causes as well as to their alma mater, The University of Akron. They provided the lead donations to build InfoCision Stadium and also establish The Taylor Institute for Direct Marketing in the College of Business Administration. The Taylor family's significant financial support has helped make a difference and created opportunity for the next generation of students at The University of Akron."

*See Appendix for more information about The Gary L. and Karen S. Taylor Institute for Direct Marketing at The University of Akron, Ohio.*

## Diversity

Create an inclusive workplace. It should go without saying that we need to be hiring people of all backgrounds and perspectives. A fully integrated workforce is more effective and sends a clear message that the business operates from the principles of respect and tolerance.

Are you looking for talented individuals with disabilities to engage with you in your business? Diversity programs should be focused on creating an environment to include those who have any number of disabilities.

**Steve:**

"Over the years I have found great success in working with state and local rehabilitation agencies to identify individuals with sight and hearing disabilities. There are a number of simple accommodations you can provide in the workplace to make it easy for these employees to successfully integrate into your business. I have found most of the time those with disabilities work harder; they are incredibly appreciative to be given an opportunity and will be loyal to your business. The government agencies provide support and training for you as an employer, and often supply resources for any needed accommodations."

**Inspire Creativity and Innovation**

Develop initiatives for employees and customers to provide feedback.

<u>Out of the Box Suggestions</u>

If you want to get employees to think out-of-the-box, you need to motivate them with some form of rewards. Moreover, suggestions have to be taken seriously so that employees are willing to come up with more creative ways of improving the workplace. Otherwise, everyone will think it's a waste of time to squeeze out creative juices for suggestions that won't be implemented anyway.

<u>Shadow Sessions</u>

Zappos allows employees to explore different interests through shadow sessions. Customer loyalty team members can schedule shadow sessions to learn about different areas of the business. They can meet with various team members to get an idea of what a typical day is like in training, merchandising, marketing, technology, or finance. This does a few things, including fostering personal connections, identifying potential talent, and allowing employees to learn and pursue new career paths at Zappos. It also gives customer facing employees a better sense of the overall values of the organization.

## Follow the Starbucks Five Ways of Being

Starbucks provides all new employee partners with The Green Apron Book, which is a short pamphlet explaining the main tenants of their corporate philosophy.

<u>The Five Ways of Being</u>

- Be Welcoming
- Be Genuine
- Be Considerate
- Be Knowledgeable
- Be Involved

Steve:

"I was out of town for a meeting and stopped by Starbucks to get coffee as I had a few minutes to spare. I was second in line and anxious to start enjoying my Venti Flat White. The server was talking with the customer ahead of me for what seemed like a few minutes and I suddenly was in a hurry. Then I overheard a small part of the conversation. She was encouraging the man who clearly was a regular, repeat customer. He was sharing the results of his recent cancer treatments. I immediately was taken back by the rapport she had developed with him (and a bit ashamed of my own impatience). Her caring attitude not only made a difference to him, but I have to say endeared me even more to the brand. Starbucks really does mean what it says and its team walked the walk that day in my clear view."

## Surround Your Customers with the Right Kind of People

Negative thinking is always counterproductive. Do your employees get together and talk about their problems or concerns in the workplace? Even worse, are they sharing negative experiences with customers? Have you had someone share with you concerns about their boss or co-workers while they were waiting on you in a restaurant or store? Creating a positive work environment involves speaking positively from the top-down, creating open door policies so employees with legitimate issues will speak with you directly and not each other to get them resolved. Sometimes it takes removing a negative person from your company completely. You cannot let it fester as the effect will carry over to other employees and customers are impacted by negative vibes.

**Customers do not want to be associated with a company where people are not genuinely happy with their work.**

A bad apple spoils the whole bunch. Remove it and you will enjoy the fruits of your labor.

Everyone on your team must have an appreciation for the best interests of the members of society in general. Sincere consideration for each individual will help you *Take Your Customer Care™ to the Next Level.*

Chapter Ten

# MEETING THE NEEDS OF MOBILE CUSTOMERS

*"Mobile has completely changed the way we interact with the world, from the way we consume and spread information to the ways we work and interact with each other. It's changed our behavior forever and raised our expectations for the brands we interact with. It has made our world more connected, more real-time, and more convenient than ever before. It has driven us to expect relevant information whenever we want it, on whatever device we want. Today, we don't just interact with connected smartphones and tablets, but with connected cars, thermostats, gaming consoles, and more. For consumers, this means experiences that are more personalized, that are context-aware, and that are delivered in real time." – "The Modern Marketer's Guide to Mobile," Oracle*

Customers today are increasing their response time requirements as smartphones, tablets, broadband connections, and services like Uber have created an on-demand society where content and services are always available 24/7/365.

**The Main Screen**

Mobile devices are becoming the main screen for consumers and are taking their attention away from their PC's and TV's.

77 percent of tablet owners use them as a so-called "second screen" while watching TV, according to a May 2014 eMarketer piece.

38 percent of consumers never disconnect from their smartphones, and 89 percent of adults check their smartphones at least several times per day, according to the 2015 Bank of America Trends in Consumer Mobility report.

**Immediate Gratification is the New Norm for Customer Care™**

Communicating effectively and seamlessly across multiple channels and devices requires an understanding of the technology that will enable you to deliver *Next Level Customer Care™ Solutions*.

Session initiation protocol, or SIP, creates the ability to combine data, video, and voice together on a single line or trunk into your technology solution. The result is lower costs and better reliability in serving your customers over any channel they choose. And customers are choosing mobile for a myriad of daily activities, from ordering dinner to setting their home thermostat, all from the latest and greatest smartphone.

**Is Your Website Mobile Friendly?**

Mobile-friendly means that text on the page is optimized for mobile devices. The text is easy to read, links/buttons are easy to select, and pages are easy to navigate on a smaller, touch-enabled screen. Using responsive design allows your site to provide the optimal viewing experience, regardless of device.

Keep It Simple to Navigate

Remember, mobile screens are much smaller to navigate than desktop and laptop screens so only give essential information you need to make the user experience pleasant and clear. Too much information can be distracting and frustrating to a viewer on such a small screen.

## Make it Easy to Scroll

Use checkable boxes and scrolling menu bars to simplify the data entry process. Make action buttons a little bigger for easy navigation with fingers.

## Choose Legible Font Size

The goal should be to draw the average viewer in with easily legible text, eliminating the need to zoom in on the screen. You don't want your viewer squinting to read text or unable to discern the letters so use at least a 14 point font size.

## Use Small Talk

Keep your text short, sweet and to the point. Make it catchy. Create memorable phrases that your audience can easily tweet out and repost. You can also include a short testimonial from a satisfied customer.

## Scale It

There are more than 500 different screen sizes between Android devices, the iPhone, Windows devices, the BlackBerry and tablets.

- Make sure your page scales to both landscape and portrait views.
- Avoid using Flash video because it does not load on iPads and iPhones.
- Create your mobile site in HTML5.

On April 21, 2015, owners of websites not optimized for mobile found they dropped to the bottom on Google's search rankings or were not even noticed at all. In a press release announcing the changes, Google stated: "Starting April 21, we will be expanding our use of mobile-friendliness as a ranking signal. This change will affect mobile searches in all languages worldwide and will have a significant impact in our search results. Consequently, users will find it easier to get relevant, high quality search results that are optimized for their devices." Google provides a mobile friendly test tool to analyze any URL and report if the page has a mobile-friendly design.

**What about Wearables?**

Mobile Marketer reports that the wearables market will grow to have annual value of about $80 billion by 2020. "Forty percent of online consumers in the United States say they are tired of pulling phones from their pockets and purses, suggesting that more mobile time will be spent in quick glances to the wrist as smartwatches catch on."

Director of Ecommerce Research at Elastic Path, Linda Busto writes: "Wearable devices are about glanceable content. This includes Google Glass, Apple Watch, fitness bands, etc. While many brands won't even bother creating experiences for these devices, every marketer should at a minimum be concerned about the smartwatch's impact on email consumption. How will your messages be best consumed by these devices?"

Global smartwatch shipments are expected to grow from 4.6 million units in 2014 to more than 28 million units in 2015, according to Strategy Analytics. Most of the smartwatch growth will come from the new Apple iWatch. "With Apple iWatch, mobile marketing and commerce will require very concise and personalized messages," said Andrew Lau of ElasticPath. "The limited user interface and personal nature of these devices will challenge marketers who are used to inundating consumers with emails, ads and impressions. The watch itself is best used to provide contextual data to the underlying mobile app to further personalize interactions."

## Mobile is Personal

Forty-four percent of cellphone users reportedly sleep with their phones next to their bed so they don't miss a message, call or update, according to Pew Research.

Because mobile devices are so personal, marketers need to be thoughtful about how they deliver marketing messages. Marketo suggests: "Consumers are looking for communication that is personalized and marketers must deliver or risk being seen as an interruption or deleted. Essentially, successful mobile marketing is about trust and relevance."

## Mobile Is Becoming Essential to Survival

We are using smartphones daily in nearly every aspect of our lives. According to The Pew Research Center from a survey in December 2014, 64 percent of American adults now own a smartphone of some kind, up from 35 percent in the spring of 2011. Smartphone ownership is especially high among younger Americans, as well as those with relatively high income and education levels. And for a number of Americans, smartphones serve as an essential connection to the broader world of online information.

The survey measured reliance on smartphones for online access in two different ways — first, by asking smartphone owners whether or not they have traditional broadband service at home, and second, whether they have a reasonable number of options for accessing the Internet in general from any location. It found that:

- 10 percent of Americans own a smartphone but do not have any other form of high-speed Internet access at home beyond their phone's data plan.
- Using a broader measure of the access options available to them, 15 percent of Americans own a smartphone but say that they have a limited number of ways to get online other than their cell phone.

## There's an App for That

Consumers can easily download the app for their favorite brands and interact to make purchases, discover new information, and share with their friends. According to Statista, in 2014, app downloads exceeded 179 billion and by 2017, the number is expected to rise to nearly 270 billion. Apps are a form of advertising that many people actually welcome on their phones, whether by downloading free options or paying for them. Companies are using apps in many ways, such as providing new services, tools or games to extend their brand; creating a mobile site so their customers have easier access to their offering or; serving up mobile banner ads to reach their target on the go.

## All Apps Are NOT Created Equal

Peter Eckert, co-founder of software company projekt202, writes: "Keeping pace with competitive pressures, companies are spending billions of dollars every year developing and deploying mobile apps that do not meet user needs and aspirations or make an emotional connection, wasting at least 30 percent of the overall spend. Apps have evolved to create a powerful brand and user experience. Good apps enable users to do things rapidly, more efficiently, and fulfill a need that in return creates an emotional bond and affinity toward a brand. Users quickly become extremely frustrated with poor apps, leading to a loss in sales and an erosion of brand value."

## App-Centricity

Erik Linask, group editorial director at TMC states: "We are undeniably being launched on a path to app-centricity. Today, if there isn't an app for something you seek to accomplish; there likely soon will be, as businesses in every vertical have realized the way to a customer's wallet is through his smartphone."

There is a shift of mobile apps from an optional component of the customer engagement cycle to a necessity in creating *Next Level Customer Care*™ in your interactions. If not properly executed though, you will alienate customers and prospects with poor app experiences. A recent CA Technologies survey, conducted by Zogby Analytics, found that 68 percent of consumers expect applications to load in six seconds or less. More than half of those, however, consider three seconds or less to be an acceptable load time. The message is simple: Make sure your app loads quickly, or you'll push users away quickly.

**Location, Location, Location**

For consumers, location-based mobile marketing is becoming routine. According to Diane Pease, inbound marketing manager for Cisco, "74 percent of adults use smartphones to get directions or information based on their current location, and 72 percent of consumers will respond to calls to action in marketing messages they receive if they are in sight of the retailer. Creating paid search ads with incentives can increase customer loyalty."

**Mobile Engagement Solutions**

Beacons

Beacons are devices that communicate with a shopper's smartphone in the hopes of improving the in-store shopping experience. When placed in a store, beacons use Bluetooth technology to detect nearby smartphones and send them media such as ads, coupons or product information. They can also be used as point-of-sale systems and to collect information on those consumers — particularly how consumers maneuver through stores.

According to Digiday, the projected benefits are two-fold: the ability to message consumers while they're in stores, and the ability to collect consumer data. Retailers hope that pushing ads and coupons to consumers while they're browsing the store aisles will induce them to buy and combat showrooming, the consumer practice of researching products in stores only to buy them later on e-commerce platforms like Amazon.

Target announced it will begin testing beacon technology this summer in a limited number of stores nationwide to provide personalized recommendation and savings. The company plans to focus on customers who have installed the latest version of the Target iPhone app and have Bluetooth activated.

## Geofencing

Geofencing is a location-based service that sends messages to smartphone users who enter a defined geographic area. "All you need is an app and GPS coordinates," says Tony Costa, an analyst at Forrester Research. But he says geofencing is immature because most companies haven't yet integrated it with their CRM systems.

## QR Codes

A QR code (quick response code) is a type of 2D bar code that is used to provide easy access to information through a smartphone. Some brands and retailers have given QR codes a try. But QR codes haven't taken off because using them is a hassle for consumers. They involve the individual having to download a QR app, take a usable picture of the QR code, and then wait for the app to deliver an offer or content – which is usually just a link to the company's website.

## Tapcentive

Tapcentive is offering an in-store mobile engagement platform that CEO Dave Wentker says is better than beacons and QR codes, because it invites customers to participate rather than pushing messages to them, and is extremely easy for shoppers to use and enjoy.

The hardware looks like a buzzer you might find in a board game. A merchant could place one or more of the "magic buttons" at the entrance to a store, a store aisle end cap, or any other spot where it is trying to draw traffic. Shoppers are encouraged to lay their smartphones on top of the button (first to get the retailer's app and subsequently) to receive store loyalty points, a discount, a gift card, or some other incentive. Wentker emphasizes the devices are not for use at the point of sale, but rather can be put at key points in the store where retailers would like on-site visitors to spend extra time.

"It's like the blue light special of the old days. It's simple," says Wentker, referring to how Kmart used to deploy a blue flashing light and make an announcement over its public address system to get shoppers to rush to a certain part of the store to get a limited-time deal.

## **Amazon Retail Stores?**

Jason Del Rey of Re/code reported in March 2015 that Amazon was considering a foray into the realm of brick-and-mortar stores: "A recently filed patent application by Amazon reveals details about a new kind of retail establishment that would allow shoppers to pick items and leave without stopping at a cashier station or kiosk. Based around the idea of complete convenience, such a store would work using a system of cameras, sensors or RFID readers that would be able to identify shoppers and the items they've chosen, according to the application, which was filed in September 2014 and published in January. The technology would also potentially give Amazon a more cost-effective way to compete with traditional retailers by operating a store that doesn't require cashiers and could similarly serve as a place to pick up online orders."

Amazon is also reportedly developing a drive-up store concept in California, according the Silicon Valley Business Journal, for shoppers to pick up grocery items they would order online.

## Don't Be a Pushover

"If the online marketing world is becoming cluttered with fluffy content, the mobile marketing space is becoming saturated with apps sitting in smartphone purgatory," according to Annum Munir at marketing and analytics app provider Localytics. "This is the part of your phone where apps you downloaded long ago sit in silence, unremembered and unused. Safe to say, it's not a place any mobile marketer wants their app to be. Today, we have the power to fight forgetfulness and stay top of mind on the one device customers always keep within reach – their phones. And that power is in push messaging."

Munir explains: "Push messages are short messages that appear on a smartphone user's home screen when he or she is not actively using your app. Push messaging should be like that polite tap on your shoulder from a friend you haven't seen in a while: immediate, personal, and re-engaging not intrusive or irrelevant."

Make it Easy to Opt In and Out of Push Notifications

Ask people to opt in to push notifications either when an app is initially downloaded, when the app is first used, or when updates are loaded. Be transparent about what content and notifications your app will send to build trust with your user. Also make it easy to opt out of push notifications or risk annoying customers.

Don't Over-Message

Don't break users' trust by being send-happy with your alerts—or else they might turn them off altogether. Be strategic about what's helpful to them.

Segment, Don't Blast

Everyone doesn't need to know everything. Offer segmented push messages that allow users to opt-in to message categories—increasing engagement with those who care and saving frustration for those who don't.

Make Messages Easy to Find

Offer a message inbox, to let users read any of your messages when they choose to do so. If a customer requests for the Starbucks App NOT to send push messages, they can still login to look for offers.

Responsys found that approximately 68 percent of smartphone users have enabled push notifications for apps, so proper execution is key in pushing information without your customers feeling as if they are being pushed over and out.

**Mobile Mind Shift**

Online fashion retailer Gilt has benefitted from the steadily increasing trend of people purchasing products directly from mobile devices. Yonatan Feldman, vice president of engineering and mobility for Gilt, was featured at Mobile Marketing Day 2015. He stated that Gilt operates from a mobile-first philosophy, thinking first about how a new feature will look on mobile and then building it for desktop, rather than the other way around to ensure "fast, simple and fun" for consumers. Brands should think of mobile as an integral part of the omnichannel experience rather than as an afterthought.

**On Average, Consumers Check Their Mobile Devices 150 Times a Day, according to Kleiner Perkins Caufield & Byers**

Greg Stuart, CEO of the Mobile Marketing Association, said: "Nothing gets marketers closer to consumers than mobile. There is no other platform that is as personal, as pervasive, and provides the opportunity for proximity."

## TO TEXT or NOT TO TEXT

The technical term for text messaging is SMS or short message service, which uses standardized communications protocols to allow landline or mobile phone devices to exchange short text messages.

Multimedia messaging service or MMS, is a standard way to send messages that include multimedia content to and from mobile phones. It extends SMS capability that allowed the exchange of text messages only up to 160 characters in length. The most popular use is to send photographs from camera-equipped handsets. It is also used by media companies as a method of delivering news and entertainment content and by retail brands as a tool for delivering scannable coupon codes, product images, videos and other information. Unlike text only SMS, commercial MMS can deliver a variety of media including up to 40 seconds of video, one image, multiple images via slideshow or audio plus unlimited characters.

According to SinglePoint, a full-service mobile technology and marketing provider, 90 percent of the time, mobile users open text messages within 90 seconds of receiving them. There are many text message marketing services to help businesses connect with customers and create two-way communication. You can alert your loyal customers about deals and specials. You can develop your relationship with your customers by creating a stronger sense of brand loyalty. Since consumers must provide you with contact information and consent to receive messages, chances are that they will be much more likely to respond positively.

The Do's and Don'ts of text message mobile marketing must include the fact that this type of marketing is permission-based ONLY. You should always be completely transparent about your text marketing program to consumers and always get everything in writing from your marketing partner.

## Two-Way Street

Currently, businesses commonly use the text channel to send one-way communications, such as widespread marketing messages or to post reminders. Customers want more, however. They want to be able to text the company back immediately with a response or to initiate a text conversation themselves. According to a 2014 Harris Poll, when questioned, customers indicated they were interested in doing a number of different activities through text—from simple tasks such as refilling orders to more complex tasks like asking questions for tech support.

The Harris Interactive 2014 U.S. Survey identified the activities people with text capabilities would most prefer to do via text:

- 38 percent check order status
- 32 percent schedule or change appointments
- 31 percent make or confirm reservations
- 30 percent ask a question
- 30 percent find a store location
- 30 percent check balances or due dates
- 29 percent refill orders
- 27 percent reset password

## Do Your Customers' Texts Go Unanswered?

If a tree falls in the woods and no one is there to hear it, does it make a sound? What about if a customer texts a company at a number that's not text enabled? The answer to the first question remains a matter of debate. The result in both cases, however, is essentially the same: It ends up on the floor.

That may be the natural order of things in the forest, but in the business environment it's not a healthy situation. Some people prefer to send instant messages rather than talk on the phone, so businesses without the ability to receive and respond to those text messages are losing out on valuable opportunities to build customer loyalty and generate new business, says TSG Global CEO Noah Rafalko.

The challenge, however, is that businesses are being inundated with an array of new technologies, and adapting to all the different channels through which customers want to communicate can be a real challenge. Green-bot is a cloud solution that helps businesses capture and respond to messages from an array of sources, and to do it in an auditable way. It works across all channels – including Facebook, Twitter, and all the various flavors of SMS and text messages – and creates a funnel to let businesses deal with such communications in a consistent and integrated way.

Contact centers can leverage Green-bot to alert agents and managers that a chat is waiting, and to notify customers who text in requests that their communications have been received and that the contact center is locating an agent with whom they can chat. It also can present details to receiving agents about why the customer sent the text, and it can pick up on key words and trigger events or automated responses based on those words.

"You know what it's like to call a business and wait on hold," Rafalko comments, "but your kids won't." Instead, they will leverage services and technologies like texting to send out their requests and go about their business while those on the receiving end of their inquiries seek solutions.

There's also an important compliance angle to Green-bot, which is especially important for such verticals as financial and medical. Green-bot and TSG recently engaged with a financial organization that wanted its brokers to be able to text for work purposes but couldn't allow it because the organization's wireless service provider wouldn't provide the necessary information to create an audit trail for this practice. However, Green-bot and TSG enabled the business to once again allow its brokers to text. That was possible because Green-bot keeps a record of everything that is said in text messages.

## Brands Can "Kik" Start Chats

Kik Messenger is an instant messaging application for mobile devices. The app is available on most phone operating systems free of charge. Kik allows advertisers to set up official accounts which chat with users through automated bots. Those brands then pay Kik to get access to more users. Kik has added the ability to target followers by gender, geography and mobile device in an effort to position itself as a more-brand friendly alternative to Snapchat. The company said in early 2015 it has more than 60 brands in the program. More than 10 million users have opted into a conversation with a brand and exchanged more than 250 million total messages. For example, users sent more than 1.7 million messages to Seventeen magazine in the first six months.

## Are Your Communications Unified?

Lucy Holloway of Evolve Media LLC, writing for Business2Community said: "Many businesses...have been slow to expand their online customer service strategy into mobile platforms, unaware of the impact this could have on customer experience. Should access to web self-service not be mobile friendly, live chat not be available on tablets or smartphones and websites not have a dedicated responsive design for mobile or tablet viewing, customers are likely to get frustrated, give up or resort to more costly channels, such as voice to resolve their query."

At this point, if they have to abandon an online transaction and call, there's a good bet that they'll have to start all over again with the transaction. And that's a quick and easy way to lose a customer or potential customer for life. Instead, companies should be helping customers get live help if they need it from inside the mobile transaction already in progress. This can be achieved through click-to-call or click-to-chat functions that carry the information from the existing transaction to call center agents, who can resolve the problem without forcing the customer to start all over again.

Art Rosenberg, writing for No Jitter, calls what companies should be chasing after UC&C capabilities, or unified communications and collaboration. "Highlighting collaboration and information content exchange as supported by persistent multimodal UC offerings is a good thing," he wrote. "However, organizations also must now include the ability for mobile customers to contact them by flexible click-for-assistance options, including instant messaging, voice, and video, depending on the situation and personal preferences."

**Mobile Moments**

A mobile moment is a point in time and space when someone pulls out a mobile device to get what he or she wants immediately, in context. Forrester Research explains, "Mobile moments redefine every customer relationship. If a customer wants information or service in a mobile moment, that is your moment to shine. Be there, and your customers will come to depend on you, deepening their loyalty and providing valuable information that your company can use to further improve the relationship. To succeed in your customer's mobile moments, you must understand their journey and identify their needs and context at each potential moment. Then design your mobile application to quickly provide just what's needed in that moment."

**Mobile Video Enables Participation**

According to Vivoom: "In today's world, participatory marketing gets the highest response rates on mobile. It's what consumers respond to, and what Millennials expect. Today's consumers want to be marketed to on their terms. They want to participate, become part of the brand experience, co-create, and share with their friends."

- 92 percent of consumers say they trust earned media, such as word of mouth from friends above all other forms of advertising, according to Nielson Research

- 75 percent of YouTube users say: "If there is a brand I love, I tell everyone about it," according to Google Research
- On YouTube, user videos get 10 times more views than brand-owned content, according to reelseo

## Mobile Enables the Next Big Thing

Mobile World Congress (MWC) convenes in the spring of each year in Barcelona. Mark Holden, head of futures at Arena Media, presented at the 2015 event. "The shift at MWC I've seen this year is a greater degree of new services and connected pieces of hardware that are enabled by a smartphone, said Holden. "This is the 'muscle' of mobile: how it is starting to shape financial services, transport, the home, leisure – and of course our experience of brands and marketing."

Holden gave several examples: "Ford, which has long been involved in the development of connected cars, is starting to build mobile services that shape transport more broadly, such as car-sharing platforms or connected bicycles that communicate with connected cars to improve road safety for both sets of users. And Peel, originally a remote control app for TV's, is extending the platform so that it becomes a remote control for connected technology across the home – solving the obvious problem that end users might not want half a dozen separate apps for half a dozen separate connected in-home pieces of technology."

Holden suggests companies consider the future of mobile platforms, personalization and devices, "think about how mobile will enable the development of new services that will make customer experiences better, and therefore create more valuable customers – not just how we take marketing messages to people."

Organizations that master the connections with customers through mobile channels will truly be able to *Take Their Customer Care™ to the Next Level* today and into the next generation.

## Chapter Eleven

# SOCIAL MEDIA AND THE PUBLIC AIRING OF CUSTOMER GRIEVANCES

*Learn from Specific Case Studies:
Who Is Doing it Right?
Who Is Doing it Wrong?
Why and Why Not?*

**<u>No company is secure today from the potential of customers holding your brand image hostage on social media due to employee malfeasance and poor judgement.</u>**

### Falling Domino's

Who can forget the infamous Domino's pizza video from 2009? A North Carolina employee posted a prank video online of another employee making sandwiches being prepared for delivery while putting cheese up his nose, mucus on the sandwiches and engaging in other disgusting health code violations. Within two days the video had been viewed more than a million times on YouTube. The company didn't even have a Twitter account until later that week and didn't respond online until the damage to customer perception had already been done.

## Ask Papa John

Fast forward to 2015 and another pizza chain employee makes a big mistake. Hip-hop star Iggy Azalea was extremely dissatisfied with her Papa John's experience the same weekend of her appearance at The Grammy Awards. The delivery employee with access to her personal phone number apparently shared it without permission. She started receiving text messages from a fan who claimed to be the delivery driver's family member.

Being an extremely popular celebrity, Azalea announced to her 4.2 million Twitter followers a few hours before the Grammy broadcast:

"Papa Johns was my favorite pizza, but the drivers they use give out your personal phone number to their family members."

Even more shocking was the flippant response the company offered referencing the title to one of Azalea's hit songs, *Bounce*.

"#WE should have known better. Customer and employee privacy is important to us. Please don't #BOUNCE us."

It seemed the company was not handling her situation any better offline as the tone of her exchange escalated over the next few days, represented by her tweets of exasperation.

"I just want answers & they have none"

"When an employee steals information it's called data breach. It's illegal. There are steps a corporation is supposed to follow afterward."

She requested a picture of the driver, and the company refused.

A Papa John's supervisor told Azalea later in a text that the employee was "on his way home to speak with his parents and sister" apparently to tell her to stop sending texts. Beyond this the company neither offered Azalea nor the public following the exchange in the Twittersphere anything resembling empathy or acknowledgement of a terrible lapse in acceptable behavior by the driver.

Eventually the company issued a statement posted by The Hollywood Reporter, "Privacy of our customers and employees is extremely important to us," it said. "Papa John's has taken appropriate disciplinary action with regard to the employee involved. We are reaching out to Ms. Azalea and hope to resolve this incident and make it right."

Whether the company made it right or not, it lost big time in the court of public opinion. Azalea announced she has moved her business to Pizza Hut and is encouraging her legion of fans to follow.

**Fly the Friendly Skies?**

The pizza business is not alone in the world of poor social customer experiences. The airline industry has some stinkers too.

Hasan Syed used Twitter's self-service ad platform to post a promoted tweet, which read: "Don't fly @British_Airways. Their customer service is horrendous." Syed, a hair-care entrepreneur based in Chicago, had flown business class on the airline with his father on a trip to Paris. When BA lost his father's luggage and failed to respond to his complaint on Twitter, he took matters into his own hands. Syed spent more than $1,000 on his smear campaign and his angry tweets were seen by more than 50,000 Twitter users in the U.K. and New York markets where his promoted tweet ran.

## US Airways

In April of 2015, US Airways mistakenly tweeted a link to a pornographic image of a naked woman with a scale model airplane, in response to at least two separate customers' complaints about the airline's service. Later that same day, the company explained that the image in question had been originally posted to its Twitter feed, and in the process of flagging the post for removal, it was inadvertently copied into the replies to the customers.

One hour later, @USAirways posted a tweet apologizing for the graphic image, announcing it was "investigating" the matter. Within 24 hours, the tweet gained more than 13,500 retweets and 10,500 favorites. Many Twitter users replied to @USAirways with jokes about the image. National media outlets carried the story that will forever live in infamy.

## American Airlines

The airline's reputation on Twitter has suffered due to robotic responses. It was reported that American Airlines responds positively to almost any tweet received. This became apparent when Ross Sheingold of social media agency, Laundry Service, sent a tweet calling AA, "the largest, sh---iest airline in the world." Sheingold had noticed that @AmericanAir thanked a guy named Mark Murphy for his support when he had really bashed the airline on its merger with US Airways. Clearly this reinforces the danger of unattended automatic tweeting.

## And Then There's JetBlue

JetBlue is the polar opposite of these airlines when it comes to excellent online customer experiences.

Lindsay Kolowich of HubSpot Blogs interviewed Laurie Meacham, JetBlue's manager of customer commitment, on the company's dedicated approach to Twitter for customer care. "We're all about people," Meacham said, "and being on social media is just a natural extension of that. It's no different than any other part of the airline."

Kolowich gives a great example to illustrate what Meacham said: "In January 2014, a man named Alex tweeted at JetBlue asking about [its] standby policy -- namely, why he would be charged $50 for getting on an earlier flight than the one he was ticketed for." Within three minutes, JetBlue replied that the $50 charge was for a confirmed seat as per its same day change policy and explained that standby is only allowed for a flight prior to the one a customer books. The airline then sent an airport employee out to talk directly with Alex, who was able to recognize him from the photo on his Twitter profile.

JetBlue has certainly dealt with crises like any other airline. Meacham told Kolowich that she talks about it with her team frequently. "Social media is powerful and things can go south so quickly, so we talk to the team all the time about how to respond appropriately, when to blow the whistle, when to contact corporate communications."

JetBlue maintains a 79.1 percent on-time arrival rate, and a customer complaint rate of just 0.79 out of every 1,000 passengers which makes it an industry leader. JetBlue has received 10 consecutive J.D. Power awards for "Highest in Customer Satisfaction Among Low-Cost Carriers in North America."

## Design a Social Media Engagement Solution to Protect from Viral Customer or Employee Negative Online Rants

Pre-Facebook, companies often ignored people they considered to be more trouble than they were worth. The squeaky wheel would eventually get greased, but was often not a top-level priority. Today, the paradigm has shifted. Unhappy consumers can hold your brand hostage and can cause you legitimate pain. Social media is a great tool for fanning flames. Those flames can signal the ship is sinking, or they can be fireworks to celebrate the relationships you are building with customers. Create opportunities for customers to speak up online as brand ambassadors. Cultivate your online brand image. Become active and vocal yourself in creating an online conversation reacting to the good and bad being said. Leave it to chance and prepare to die.

**When employees are empathetic, engaged, and empowered, the customer experience is elevated. When customers are put on a pedestal and happy with you and your product solutions, you are pre-mitigating the majority of concerns with complaints.**

**However we never live in a utopian world, so we must prepare for inevitable misunderstandings that may arise.**

**Are Your Ears Burning?**

Let's face it, people are talking about you online, but wouldn't you like to know who, when and to whom, so you could join in the conversation?

According to a 2013 study by J.D. Power, 67 percent of consumers reported that they had used a company's social media site for servicing. This means you had better be prepared to treat social media channels just as you would any other customer contact media. It's important that companies build a timely way to respond to consumer posts. It takes focus, effort and strategy to perfect your social media response protocols, but getting in the game will at least ensure you're not missing important complaints in public forums, where the danger of being the last to know is high.

A study done by Simply Measured showed that 99 percent of brands are on Twitter and 30 percent of them have a dedicated customer service handle. The average response time was 5.1 hours with 10 percent of companies answering within one hour and 93 percent within 48 hours.

Starbucks uses Facebook and Twitter effectively for customer feedback. It is active in sharing information and quick to respond to customer questions and complaints. Starbucks seems to have mastered the art of bringing balance to its postings. Its brand personality shines while still keeping sensitivity when a legitimate concern is voiced. Starbucks also started a separate Twitter account called @MyStarbucksIdea for customers to share recommendations to make Starbucks better.

With more than 34 million Facebook fans, Walmart has a big job just keeping up with customer interactions. It posts many updates and timely replies. Even the toughest complaints are met with a polite and sincere response. It strives to address the issues publicly but will direct them to special handling team members. Walmart's Facebook Feedback Tab is powered by the GetSatisfaction support tool, which provides the ability to not only respond to routine customer feedback and questions, but to also quickly share important updates such as product recalls. Walmart does have a corporate Twitter account, but the primary response sends customers to its Facebook Feedback Tab.

**Do You Surprise and Delight Your Customers?**

Social media is a great forum for showcasing your efforts to let customers know you value them as individuals. We all love to be surprised with an unexpected gift of appreciation.

Scott Matthews, CEO of CrowdTwist shared in Advertising Age: "brands are making this customer service tactic, commonly called 'surprise and delight,' far less random, and in some cases, it's the driving force behind several nationwide, multimillion-dollar marketing campaigns."

MasterCard

MasterCard launched a program called Priceless Surprises, connecting with members on social media to give them spontaneous gifts and prizes, like a meeting with Justin Timberlake, an exclusive Gwen Stefani concert, or even VIP tickets to the Grammy Awards. By engaging its customers with genuinely surprising gifts and experiences, and leveraging these fans to reach new potential customers, the campaign serves to create loyal existing customers while bringing on new ones as well.

Bud Light

Bud Light generated massive buzz during the 2014 Super Bowl with its #UpForWhatever campaign. A random Bud Light drinker was rewarded for being "Up for Whatever" with a spontaneous, star-studded, unforgettable night out. To build on the success, Bud Light created the fictional place "Whatever, USA" in Montana and held auditions for fans to win a weekend of concerts and fun. The event was streamed in real time as 1,200 winners experienced the big party. Bud Light created a unique website to continually share information and updates on new opportunities for customers to join in on the next adventure. The viral effect has been to develop a growing community of Bud Light loyalists.

Matthews recommends: "Whether you decide to send a small surprise to customers in the mail, or treat them to a weekend full of partying, embracing elements of surprise and delight into your loyalty strategy will drive emotional connections and create long-term customers and brand advocates."

## Nike is a Great Example of Social Customer Experience Excellence

Nike uses a dedicated customer care Twitter account (@NikeSupport) to handle customer inquiries and within a three month period receives approximately 40,000 mentions. Nike responds to customers, on average, within 2.8 hours—55 percent of replies are returned in less than 30 minutes.

Social media's transparency has changed the customer relationship landscape and there is no turning back. Daily Finance reported that 47 percent of consumers on social media actively seek customer support via social channels.

Start listening on Twitter, and see what people are saying about your company (Hootsuite makes this really easy).

Zappos reputation for its Customer Care™ is legendary. It was widely reported when a Zappos' employee helped a father find a shoe for his daughter. The communication occurred completely on Twitter as the employee became aware of the man's needs by searching the web.

## **Where Do You Start in Developing a Social Customer Experience?**

### **Respond Quickly**

People are looking for real-time information. It's important to get back to questions and concerns in a timely manner.

### Always On

Social media is always open for business, 24 hours per day, seven days per week, 365 days each year, and you shouldn't be caught asleep at the switch. If you are not prepared to implement an around the clock care process in-house, then find a partner to handle your after-hours service needs. Customers want more than the lights on when they stop by; they expect your response all day, every day.

### Create a One to One Experience

Enable your team to represent you in their own name which will engage customers with a personalized approach.

## Use Social Media as a Communications Channel

Share company updates, recognize customers and employees. Information should be pushed out without being sales oriented. People will reach out to you as well, and you should respond whether they are current customers or not. Being endearing is an important part of developing a relationship.

## Listen, Learn and Respond

Utilize social media analytics to capture what is being said online about your brand image.

Following are some of the most popular and FREE social-media analytics tools.

- Google Social Analytics
- Social Mention
- SumAll
- Facebook Insights
- Twitter Analytics

**Proactive Social Media Engagement**

Just having a Facebook page or Twitter account won't cut it anymore. You need to invest in your social media strategy. Use online and digital tools to build a community of dedicated customers.

Ryan Holmes, CEO of Hootsuite reported in Forbes that: "Social media has given companies access to unprecedented amounts of information on client behavior and preferences – so-called big data. But making sense of it all and turning it into actionable policy has been elusive. Larger organizations – including Gatorade, Dell and the Super Bowl, as well as the Red Cross – have led the way here, pioneering dedicated command centers for real-time monitoring and analysis.

**"Social media mission control rooms are staffed by multiple employees, the centers outfitted with banks of screens tracking everything from tweets and likes to customer sentiment."**

### Active Advocates

Customers who are loyal to a company's products or services are less likely to be drawn away to a competitor with better deals and discounts. They are product driven as opposed to price driven and tend to be engaged on a personal level. They will endorse the company to friends and family both online and offline.

**More than half of customers are more likely now than five years ago to share their experiences, according to Dimension Research.**

**"How likely is it you would recommend us to a friend?"**

Bain & Co. developed the Net Promoter Score, or NPS, based on one single question:

How likely is it you would recommend us to a friend?

Bain & Co. commented on the experience of one of its clients: "Charles Schwab spent a considerable amount of time testing its NPS metric to establish the value and integrity of the process. Schwab's researchers learned that shorter surveys brought higher response rates. [It] found that changes in the presentation of survey questions needed to be rigorously tested to ensure that they didn't introduce variation into the score. Over time, Schwab was able to develop a robust, reliable metric, customized for its needs. The team could demonstrate that the top 10 percent of branches, as measured by NPS, grew 30 percent faster, on average, than the branch network as a whole. It also found that about half of new Schwab clients listed referrals or recommendations as a primary reason for coming to Schwab."

## Can You Use Social Media to Mend and Heal a Broken Online Image?

Absolutely! Customers will usually understand if you make a mistake, own it and make amends. It is more difficult when the situation is being aired publicly. But think about it. If you show how much you care about your customer who is affected by your mistake, and you do make it right, there are numerous people listening in and watching how you handle the situation. You can use that instance to tell your story of great Customer Care™ response in spite of a failure.

Accenture noted in a report outlining social media customer experience: "One U.S. bank initiated a major change program to improve the customer experience as a means of gaining market share. The bank leveraged a crowdsourcing tool to tap into its workforce for ideas about how to improve customer service. In the first use of the tool, more than 250 employees submitted 50 separate ideas resulting in seven high-quality innovations for the company—many of which resulted in programs that have generated value for the bank."

## Turning the Tide

The telecommunications and cable industry gets more than its fair share of criticism and customer moaning. But companies like Comcast can make a difference and show they truly CARE.

<u>Comcast Vilified</u>

A July 2014 service call went viral in which one of its customer service representatives aggressively repeated questions and avoided a customer's request to cancel his service.

The customer, Ryan Block, recorded the final eight minutes of the call and posted it online. Block stated: "The representative continued aggressively repeating his questions, despite the answers given, to the point where my wife became so visibly upset she handed me the phone...This recording picks up roughly 10 minutes into the call, whereby she and I have already played along and given a myriad of reasons and explanations as to why we are canceling (which is why I simply stopped answering the rep's repeated question — it was clear the only sufficient answer was 'Okay, please don't disconnect our service after all')."

Comcast apologized profusely. "We are very embarrassed by the way our employee spoke with Mr. Block and are contacting him to personally apologize," the company said in a statement. "We are investigating this situation and will take quick action. While the overwhelming majority of our employees work very hard to do the right thing every day, we are using this very unfortunate experience to reinforce how important it is to always treat our customers with the utmost respect."

Comcast Deserves Credit

Comcast Cable President and CEO Neil Smit has publicly said that Customer Care™ is a priority for 2015. "The way we interact with our customers -- on the phone, online, in their homes -- is as important to our success as the technology we provide," Smit wrote on the company blog. "Put simply, customer service should be our best product."

Daniel B. Kline of The Motley Fool reports: "The company has put a respected company veteran in charge of repairing its broken method of interacting with customers. It has also created an app which lets people know when a technician is *enroute* to their home, instead of having to wait around during a four-hour appointment window. Now Comcast is taking its efforts to fix its customer relations a step further by hiring 40 additional workers for its social media team, 'ComcastCares.' They join an existing 20-person group in providing help with everything from scheduling appointments to troubleshooting Internet problems and setting up DVR."

Kline goes on to say: "The company deserves praise for not just saying it's going to fix the problem but actually doing the hard work to turn around its culture, while backing those efforts with financial resources. This is good business for the cable and Internet giant. Comcast deserves credit for publicly tackling what is a thankless problem. Bringing the customer service battle to social media is a smart move. Twitter and Facebook allow for quick problem resolution. That should result in happy customers and less stress on traditional phone-based customer service."

Some industries are much more difficult than others to navigate through social media turbulence. Be sure you are focused on the customer first and foremost and not taking shortcuts.

**Getting Better Reviews on Yelp**

Yelp's influence and footprint are substantial and growing. The company now feeds content and reviews to Apple Maps, Bing, and Yahoo among others. Yelp's Director of Public Policy, Luther Lowe recently announced the company would provide for "incentivized check-ins" to help generate Yelp reviews.

Greg Sterling of Search Engine Land explains: "Yelp's strict 'no review solicitation' policy has left many marketers and local business owners frustrated and even angry. And Yelp's 'review filter' practices have been the subject of lawsuits and numerous unproven conspiracy theories."

"Yelp is allowing business owners to create a pre-review reward for users, who then are asked to review that business," Sterling says. "While Yelp doesn't allow businesses to create rewards directly for reviews, this is an indirect version of that. For businesses with few Yelp reviews this appears to be a good strategy to generate reviews, which are more likely than not to be favorable — coming off the incentive or offer. Yelp partly wants business owners to encourage check-ins because it helps Yelp prove value and usage."

## Forgiven but Not Forgotten

We would all appreciate the opportunity to simply be forgiven by a customer for an incident of bad customer service and have it be forgotten. With the viral nature of social media, there are numerous examples of companies that have imploded spectacularly with a single customer service error. The apology may have been received but you can never really erase online comments.

One bad story can be on a million potential customers' mobile screens in a matter of minutes. Customers know that if they aren't treated with respect, they can make you squirm. Customers expect to have their issues resolved right now, right here, in whatever channel they choose to reach out in. This is especially true of younger consumers. Most companies simply aren't prepared to step up to that level of customer support yet. But they need to be.

The VAR Guy's Elliot Markowitz wrote that companies need to restructure themselves to address the needs of their customers in an on-the-spot way. Markowitz shares the story of a mother who went to a big box retailer to exchange an iPad mini still under warranty. The store manager replied with verbatim company policy, which dictated that the device would take 15 days to replace. "Clearly there were hundreds still in the store," wrote Markowitz. "The twist here is that the device was for an autistic child who is nonverbal and can only communicate through this device. At this point, the service manager should have taken the request to the store owner, who hopefully would realize the bigger picture by doing what is not only socially correct but also good for business."

Instead, the manager stood by company policy, and the mother blasted the company on social media, resulting in a large number of customers and disabled rights groups declaring a boycott on the retailer.

*Nadji Tehrani; Steve Brubaker*

**A customer who has been failed by a company doesn't appreciate the words "your business is important to us." Actions speak louder than words. Enable your team to take appropriate steps to treat customers with great care and empathy...**

To literally, *Go the Extra Mile!*

## Chapter Twelve

# WHAT GOES AROUND COMES AROUND... NEXT LEVEL CUSTOMER CARE™: REPUTATION MANAGEMENT AND COMPETITIVE ADVANTAGE

Customer Care™ is often considered a nasty four-letter word to some members of corporate boardrooms and shareholders. When misunderstood it is viewed as a drain on the bottom line. Rewards are given for increases in sales volume, yet advances in relationship building often go unnoticed.

It is common to hear high praise of a company's products, yet disdain for their customer service in the next breath. It is challenging at best and can consume limited resources if not executed properly.

**NO business can afford to lose customers. There is no better way to keep customers than to *Take Your Customer Care™ to the Next Level*.**

**Intense Competition Leads to Improved Customer Care™**

Companies appreciate their customers far more when there's a high chance customers will leave them and take their business elsewhere. A new survey from Ipsos found that 39 percent of respondents ranked government offices as having the worst customer service in the country. Telecommunications companies weren't far behind at 38 percent. In third place for the worst service experience was the healthcare industry at 18 percent. Many smaller communities have few choices of healthcare providers.

## Win Back

A lost customer can be redeemed. Don't give up on a customer who leaves you. According to Frederick Reichheld of Bain & Co.: "It is common for a business to lose 15 to 20 percent of its customers each year...when defections are cut in half, the average growth rate more than doubles. A 5 percent change in rate of retention swings profit increases from 25 percent all the way to 100 percent." Of course the goal is not to lose them in the first place, but don't give up and leave them to your competitors. Pursue them and ask them why they left and what would help them to reconsider. If they share a concern, listen and find a way to apologize to build trust. Then look for an opportunity to ask for their business once again.

## 360 Degree Feedback Loop

<u>So, How Did We Do?</u>

Ask for feedback to gauge customer sentiment. Share with employees. Create a 360-degree loop on customer engagement.

## Caring Means NOW...Don't Make Me Wait

## Develop an Ongoing Relationship

Steve:

"When our children were younger, my wife, Robin, and I would leave them with a family member or sitter on date night. We communicated and expected our caregiver to do everything necessary to care for our daughters."

*Taking Your Customer Care™ to the Next Level*

Next Level Customer Care™ delivers the same effect. Do whatever it takes to create a lasting impression and experience.

### Don't Put Me on HOLD and Don't HANG UP on Me!

**With consumers being pressed for time and the increased options of digital avenues for communicating with customers, most people are not willing to be on hold with a customer service department for more than one minute, according to a new survey from Velaro, a provider of live chat software.**

In a unique study that surveyed more than 2,500 consumers, nearly 60 percent of respondents believe that one-minute is too long to be on hold. In addition, 32 percent of consumers believe that customer service departments should be answering immediately – with no hold time.

"This is a clear indication that consumers are not willing to spend unnecessary time waiting on hold when calling a company," said Jeff Mason, vice president of marketing for Velaro. "Today's consumers expect an efficient interaction and are no longer willing to wait unnecessarily. This reinforces the need for companies to seek more efficient customer service solutions, such as live chat software – and the quicker, the better."

**When asked "For customer service, how long are you willing to be put on hold?" respondents answered:**

| | |
|---|---|
| None: | 32 percent |
| 1 minute: | 28 percent |
| 1-5 minutes: | 30 percent |
| 5-10 minutes: | 6 percent |
| More than 10 minutes: | 4 percent |

Craig Borowski of Software Advice notes that as much as customers dislike waiting on hold, businesses dislike it, too—they pay for all time spent on the phone, even when customers are just waiting.

He states that the obvious solution to reduce hold times is to hire more agents. But not only is this rarely a cost-effective solution, it can cause a scheduling dilemma: Having enough agents when call volume is at its peak usually means paying for many agents to sit idle when volume is low.

Software Advice conducted a survey as well to find out if and when customers appreciate callback technology. It asked respondents which they'd prefer if they called a company and all agents were busy: waiting on hold, or receiving a call back. The majority—63 percent—preferred callback.

Callback can be immediate if an agent is available at that moment. If not, however, the system can offer to put the customer on hold, while providing the likely wait time, or enable the customer to get a call back at a future time. That opens the door to helping contact centers shift their traffic patterns so they're more predictable, which can lower costs and make for an easier to manage environment, notes Tom Jameson, executive vice president of worldwide sales at Virtual Hold Technology LLC in a recent white paper.

Jameson refers to this concept as virtual queuing, which he says can be used to guide customers into scheduling callbacks during low volume intervals. That can translate into more predictable and steady call flow through the day, which makes it easier to do staff scheduling, enables contact centers to maximize their agent occupancy rates, and can allow for a better customer experience.

## 90 Percent of Customers Claim Hold Time is their Primary Cause of Frustration

Source: Virtual Hold Technology

**Despite all the new technology enabling online self-service, Oliver VanDervoort of TMC reports that 57 percent of customers in 2014 still preferred the telephone over any other method of contact.**

How much an employee interacts directly with a customer matters greatly. People are expecting your team to be able to suggest actions and answer questions even if those answers aren't routine. Having staff members that care about their jobs and the people who are your customers are two points that drive customer satisfaction to its highest level.

**Reputation Management**

Reputation management is the practice of monitoring the reputation of an individual or brand on the Internet, addressing content which is potentially damaging to it, and using customer feedback solutions to get input or early warning signals to reputation problems. Most of reputation management is focused on pushing down negative search results. Reputation management may attempt to bridge the gap between how a company perceives itself and how others view it.

**"It Takes 20 Years to Build a Reputation and Five Minutes to Ruin It. If You Think About That, You'll do Things Differently," according to Warren Buffett.**

**Google search results are the primary target of reputation management efforts. Some of the legal and ethical tactics used by reputation management firms include the following:**

- **Improving the tagging and search engine optimization of company-published materials, such as white papers and positive customer testimonials in order to push down negative content**
- **Publishing original, positive websites and social media profiles, with the aim of outperforming negative results in a search**
- **Submitting online press releases to authoritative websites to promote brand presence and suppress negative content**

- **Submitting court-ordered removal requests if someone believes they have been libeled**
- **Getting mentions of the business or individual in third-party sites that rank highly in Google**
- **Proactively responding to public criticism stemming from recent changes**

**Monitor Your Reputation**

Know what is being said about your Business; or Not

When people visit your business, they walk away with an impression. And even if they don't tell you, they might tell others what they think. They might talk about you on Twitter or Facebook. Or they might write a review of your business on Yelp, letting others know why they should or shouldn't work with you. Most likely they won't tell you that they're talking about you, so you need to find the comments for yourself. It's important to know what they are saying so that you can respond appropriately.

If you don't find anyone talking about you, that says something too. People may not be criticizing you, but they're also not singing your praises. Perhaps you aren't doing a good enough job promoting yourself, or not making a good enough impression on your customers. You want them to talk about you and the great Customer Care™ you provide. If they aren't, then look for ways to promote brand advocates.

**You DON'T want negative reviews, but you certainly DO want positive ones.**

Know What Changes to Make

No one likes getting negative feedback. We don't want to be told that our products are horrible or that our employees are rude. When you monitor your brand online and notice poor reviews, you need to listen. What if the feedback is true? What if multiple people are making the same observations? Use this feedback to make appropriate changes. Reach out to those people and let them know you are taking their criticism seriously, rather than getting defensive. Listen to what they say, and *Take Your Customer Care™ to the Next Level.*

## Know What Your Competitors are Doing

Don't just monitor your own brand; monitor your competitors. You don't want to operate out of a posture of fear and constant competition, but knowing what others are doing can be extremely helpful as you seek to move your business forward. You need to know what people are saying about your competitors. Think of it as military intelligence. If customers are unhappy with some aspect of your competitor's business, you can take advantage of that information.

## Know How to Respond

Don't let people talk about you without at least finding a way to respond. If someone is shouting your praises, thank them! Find a way to engage them. They might become some of your best brand ambassadors. If someone is criticizing you, you also need to respond. You should apologize to them even if you don't think it's your fault. You can tell them you're sorry that they had a bad experience. Reach out to them and try to make it right.

## **Customer Care™ Is Perhaps the Most Important Aspect of Social Media, and One that is Tied Directly to Marketing**

Nadji:

""Yelp Ratings have been helpful to me personally in determining whether to do business with a company. I was watching a television advertisement offering a 'free' product for diabetes patients. I decided to call to understand better what was being offered. The salesperson shared he was unable to proceed until I provided details about my personal history, including any prescribed medications."

"I also looked online at the Yelp customer testimonials. The list started off with all positive stories, which appeared not to be genuine, as if the person had been paid to write a glowing report. There was one letter though from a lady who explained she had ordered and tried to reach out for customer service. She had been put on hold and hung up on several times without ever receiving assistance. That single report was good enough for me. I was already skeptical, and her letter reinforced my decision not to continue contact. The whole process gave me the impression of a bait and switch operation.""

## Google Alerts

Google is always expanding its tools and applications, but Google Alerts is one that's actually been around for a while, and it's still one of the most effective tools for online reputation management. Set up alerts for any search terms you want, such as your company name or targeted phrases relevant to your niche, then specify the types of results you want and how often. You can even get alerts as mentions occur for real-time online reputation management. Google sends alerts directly to you in an email digest, so there's no ongoing legwork involved. And, Google Alerts is free.

## Don't Delete Negative Comments

Consultant Jonny Ross says: "This may sound like a strange tip, but it is something that many businesses do. Deleting comments won't make the problem go away. Instead, it makes your business appear to your audience as if you cannot deal with their comments. It can also have a damaging effect on your business. You can make negative comments less easy to find by ensuring you are constantly posting great, original content."

Reputation management doesn't require a full-time schedule, but you must be dedicated to monitor the pulse of activity related to your business reputation.

### Welcome Critique

**Remember that Your Best Customers are the Ones Who Criticize Your Service. Without them Your Customer Care™ Will Be Compromised."**

### Ethics in Customer Care™

Ethics are a set of principles that govern the conduct of an individual or group. There are no shortcuts when it comes to being truthful and making appropriate choices. If customers do not see individuals in business as being honest, then the company will not succeed for long.

When faced with an ethically challenging situation, ask yourself:

- Is the action legally permissible?
- Would it be fair to all involved?
- How would my family and friends react to my decision?
- How would the decision make me feel when it is said and done?

### Do the Right Thing for Customers for the Right Reasons

Everyone must win in a business decision for the partnership to last. If someone loses, then you can be sure no legacy will be created.

### Reduce Customer Experience Frustration

Bill Franks, chief analytics officer of Teradata, commented in Forbes on how airlines are increasingly using analytics to efficiently reroute planes and people when faced with a wave of delays and cancellations due to weather. He states: "Your MBA mindset would rightly have you focusing on the cost savings from more efficiently scrambling planes and crew members to the right locations to keep more planes flying and service the most passengers. But, also remember what the customer is thinking of: the delay experience itself. Was it a moderately annoying three-hour delay, with good customer service that allowed you to relax with full knowledge of how you'd be impacted; or was it a harrowing three-hour nightmare of frustrating interactions with airline staff who didn't seem to know what was going on?"

"Having analytics reroute passengers before they land is of immense value to the passengers. They can now relax and grab a drink or meal knowing what the new plan is instead of stressing while waiting in a lengthy line or on hold. Being more proactive won't fix everything for the customer, but it will make the experience as positive as possible and will leave the impression that the airline was on top of it from the start. That will lead to more loyalty."

There are some unbelievable stories about companies that don't put a concerted effort toward their quality of Customer Care™. In fact, just recently a woman spent six hours on hold with American Airlines trying to rebook her cancelled flight due to weather-related issues. Instances such as this not only frustrate customers on an individual level, but they also damage a company's reputation on a greater scale.

Giant brand-name businesses, such as American Airlines, have plenty of resources available that they should be using to establish themselves as Customer Care™ experts. One such resource, which tends to have the greatest impact, is simply the attentiveness and personality demonstrated by the employee.

Paula Bernier, executive editor of TMC spoke with ACSI inventor Claes Fornell. Claes talked about how businesses, such as airlines, could improve customer satisfaction simply by sharing information with their customers. He said: "[Businesses] should communicate what they know; information here is critical. They are very bad at this. When bad things happen, delays and the like, the airlines are getting a little better, but they're not really on top of things. They should let people know what to expect to the extent that they know it...I think they should communicate so that passengers should make other plans if they have to. And I'm still amazed in the plane itself. If you run into turbulence or whatever, the captain should say something. Sometimes they do, sometimes they don't say anything. It's not consistent."

In contrast to the American Airlines story, a customer service representative of online retailer Zappos once stayed on the line with a customer for an incredible 10 hours. The length of the interaction was not due to hold time or conflict; rather, the employee was expressing out of this world service and social skills.

Zappos exhibited quality Customer Care™ through the skills exhibited by its employee, while American Airlines' call didn't even make it to the point of contact.

**Reduce Customer Effort**

According to a survey by the Customer Contact Council, 59 percent of respondents reported expending moderate-to-high effort to resolve an issue. 62 percent of the respondents reported having to repeatedly contact a company to resolve an issue. These results clearly show that organizations need to continuously evaluate the effort their customers must use to resolve a problem or get a question answered.

**Don't Make Your Customers Repeat Themselves**

VoltDelta reports: "The annoyance meter is raised when customers are asked to repeat information after being transferred from an IVR to an agent, or between agents. Cost-effective technology will address this issue. For example, WhisperTel provides agents with a voice recording of what happened in the voice self-service channel prior to taking the call."

## Ask for Customer Feedback, but Don't Harass

Sending follow-up surveys to customers after a customer service interaction or after a purchase is a common and often helpful practice to obtain feedback. It is also useful to request comment at unexpected intervals, in a way that doesn't bother the customer but shows your company values his or her opinions. For example, sending quarterly online surveys by mail or via social media are non-invasive ways of asking for feedback just to see how the customer feels in general. The input helps a company better define goals and know where customer service improvements can be made.

Nadji:

"My wife, Julie, shared that after making a deposit recently, she received calls for several weeks on her mobile number from the bank. Usually when the calls arrived, she would be driving and would choose not to answer. The bank would leave the same message asking her to call and take a survey of her experience at the bank. Finally she called and asked to be taken off the list, as she simply preferred not to be contacted with surveys in the future."

Don't harass and continue to press for customers to complete surveys. Ask once or twice at the most and move on. You do not need or even want everyone to respond! Some people prefer not to answer and continuing to badger them will likely alienate them and could result in losing them as a customer altogether.

## Customer Surveys: Unintended Consequences

Asking customers for their feedback and listening to identify how to improve is one of the most basic Customer Care™ philosophies.

Surveys can be very useful provided they are implemented properly. Also, it is critical that surveys are not overused or too lengthy to add any element of frustration to the customer experience.

**Steve:**

"A certain national department store instructs its cashiers to tell every customer to, 'Fill out an online survey and receive a coupon for your next visit. My name is ____. Please tell them how well I did.' The staff members at this store are rarely out in the aisles assisting customers, as they are positioned at the cash registers in the center of the store. There is very little to share about the service provided. To be told to go online each and every time I make a purchase is annoying. I bristle when told to 'give them a good rating.' The practice has the opposite effect of encouraging customer appreciation."

**Employees should not be trained nor incented to push customers to rate them more highly than they naturally would.**

CFI Group reports of employees even telling customers: "You may get a survey about your experience. Please rate me as excellent, or I could lose my job."

Just saying: "Thank you for your business, I appreciate you as a customer" works far better than trying to convince people to vote for you on a survey. Do not evaluate employees based on the number of surveys returned. Instead, celebrate the individual every time you receive glowing feedback.

**Don't Poison the Well**

Receiving perfect survey scores is so important for certain companies that they resort to bribing customers with coupons or free gifts. One Pizza Hut franchisee taped a note to its pizza boxes begging for perfect scores. Instead of rewarding customers for their candid feedback, the restaurant explicitly stated that it would only provide coupons to customers who provided a 5-star review. In essence, Pizza Hut was incentivizing positive feedback and thus encouraging those with negative remarks to either lie or abstain.

The Customer Experience Impact 2010 Report found that:

- 40 percent of consumers switched to buying from a competitor because of its reputation for great customer service.
- 85 percent say they would pay 5 percent to 25 percent more to ensure a superior customer experience.
- 76 percent of US consumers say they appreciate brands that take a personal interest in them.

## Self-Help Online

Companies need to look at their websites and determine where they can provide customer service options beyond just standard marketing and sales information.

**<u>Be sure to provide a phone number for those that prefer to make the call.</u>**

## Next Level Identification: Voice Biometrics

Voiceprint identification provides a level of positive identification you never thought possible. With the continued rise of identity theft and also the desire by companies to securely help customers access information as rapidly as possible, voice biometrics has emerged as a way to answer these challenges and secure customer data.

- Financial services can authenticate callers to eliminate waiting on hold.

- Healthcare patients may receive automated status updates and prescription notifications securely.

## The Key to Customer Engagement

<u>Understand the Customer</u>

Map the entire customer experience through the various touch points of retail stores, website, social media, and contact centers. Review the information available from each interaction to identify and correct any disconnects.

- Brand Promise Fulfillment: Is every step in the customer journey matching what you are promising and more? Test, Evaluate and Take corrective action.
- R-E-S-P-E-C-T: Treat employees according to The Golden Rule and they will do the same with your customers.
- Loyalty: Long-term loyal relationships with customers are created by offering customized offers, as opposed to one size fits all discounts. Utilizing the data available provides the ability to delight customers with unique and special promotions.

## The Measurement Trap

There are as many measurements of customer satisfaction as there are consultants in the business. Some may feel the tools are unnecessary, such as the business owner who said: "We do customer research everyday by counting the money coming in the door."

Examples of popular tools are:
<u>NPS: Net Promoter Score</u>
Developed by Bain & Co., the NPS asks customers: "How likely is it that you would recommend us to a friend of colleague?"

Satmetrix's 2015 Annual Net Promoter Industry Benchmarks report ranks more than 220 brands. "Our 2015 reports provide not only industry rankings according to companies' Net Promoter Scores, but also direct insight into which customer experiences drive loyalty and are most critical to a company's success," said Brendan Rocks, head of data science at Satmetrix.

**The Satmetrix Net Promoter Benchmarks are based on survey responses from more than 30,000 U.S. consumers nationwide.**

- **Netflix took the top spot in the Online Entertainment category.**
- **Trader Joe's led the Grocery/Supermarkets sector.**
- **JetBlue won in the Airlines sector, beating out last year's winner Southwest Airlines.**
- **The Apple iPad/iPad mini finished first for Tablet Computers**
- **Ritz Carlton won for Hotels, overtaking Westin.**
- **Costco had the best overall NPS score at 79.**

NEV: Net Emotional Value

Created by Beyond Philosophy, Net Emotional Value is "a single number that represents how your customers 'on balance' feel towards you. To put it simply NEV is the net of positive emotions less negative emotions."

A simple calculation based on the Emotion Scale for NEV would be:

NEV = Average of the Positive Emotions (Happy, Pleased, Trusting, Valued, Cared for, Safe, Focused, Indulgent, Stimulated, Exploratory, Interested, Energetic) – Average of the Negative Emotions (Dissatisfied, Frustrated, Disappointed, Irritated, Stressed, Unhappy, Neglected, Hurried)

## CES: Customer Effort Score

Corporate Executive Board originated the Customer Effort Score, which is a transactional measurement to discover the amount of effort involved in resolving a customer's issue. It can help pinpoint processes that are creating more effort for your customers. Ask whether "The company made it easy for me to handle my issue."

## CSAT: Customer Satisfaction

The traditional customer satisfaction score, or CSAT as it's often called, intends to measure a customer's satisfaction with the service received. In its simplest form, CSAT is expressed as a percentage between 0 and 100, with 100 percent representing complete customer satisfaction.

CSAT is often determined by a single question in follow-up surveys: "How would you rate your overall satisfaction with the service you received?" This is often graded on a scale of one to five, with a score of one representing "very dissatisfied" and five representing "very satisfied." All surveys are then averaged for a composite CSAT score.

According to Impact Learning Systems: "This methodology doesn't take into account that many mildly satisfied or mildly dissatisfied customers don't tend to complete surveys. It also fails to differentiate specific factors that contribute to customer satisfaction such as good value (the quality and quantity of the service for its price), how closely the customer's expectations are met, and how valued the customer feels at the end of a transaction with this company."

"This lack of detail can skew CSAT results in either direction. As with other metrics, one of CSAT's most useful purposes is to track the correlation between changes in training or procedures and the satisfaction of customers. As long as the method used to measure satisfaction does not change between pre- and post- change surveys, CSAT can help companies determine the effect of new initiatives on their customers' satisfaction."

## VoC: Voice of the Customer

The Voice of the Customer is a process used to capture feedback from the customer to provide the customers with the best in class service quality. This process is all about being proactive and constantly innovative to capture the changing requirements of the customers with time.

VoC is used to describe the stated and unstated needs or requirements of the customer. The voice of the customer can be captured in a variety of ways: direct discussion or interviews, surveys, focus groups, customer specifications, observation, warranty data, field reports, complaint logs, etc.

## Benchmark Your Position Properly

Whatever tool you choose, be sure you have the ability to compare what you are doing to others in your same industry. Benchmarking is crucial for *Taking Your Customer Care™ to the Next Level*.

But be careful! Our good friend Mark Miller, contact center solutions practice leader at J.D. Power, described the benefits and pitfalls of benchmarking performance in a recent interview with CUSTOMER magazine. www.customerzone360.com

Miller stated: "A benchmarking hazard is comparing your performance against the 'average' performance of other companies. Keep in mind that 50 percent of the organizations will perform 'better than average.' Settling for better-than-average gives the false impression that you've effectively differentiated yourself when you may not have."

Miller offers these specific recommendations for effective benchmarking strategies:

## Benchmark against Others That Value the Same Service Standards as You Do

"Organizations that use J.D. Power benchmarks, value most the provision of superior service to their customers, and they balance that against their other priorities. They either currently provide, or want to provide, a differentiated experience through service. If your organization puts customers first, then benchmarking against organizations that put operational issues ahead of customers won't help you improve. Controlling costs remains an operational imperative, even among organizations that prioritize the customer experience. However, many of those organizations achieve cost controls through improvements in customer and employee retention as a result of their service orientation. Regardless of what your organization values most, benchmarking against organizations that share those values will improve your benchmarking."

## Benchmark Operational Practices, Not just Statistics

"Managing operational metrics or statistics is not enough. For example, it is insufficient to benchmark and then act on employee attrition statistics without understanding the drivers of that attrition."

**"High-performing companies benchmark at least three elements to get the whole picture:**

**(1) Customer experience (including loyalty)**
**(2) Key operational and performance metrics**
**(3) Best practices."**

## Look Outside your Industry for Top Performers

"Another critical component of effective benchmarking is to look at what high performers outside your industry do. Almost without exception, your customers' expectations are not wholly created by interactions with your competitors or even within your industry, but rather by interactions with high-performing organizations outside your industry," Miller says. "A great experience anywhere becomes the standard by which consumers judge all other experiences, and J.D. Power helps organizations meet that standard."

As we have said over and over, Customer Satisfaction is not enough. You must *Take Your Customer Care™ to the Next Level.* You do this by *"Going the Extra Mile."*

**Competitor ONE-TWO PUNCH:**

**Develop Customer Care™ as your LETHAL WEAPON of Competitive Advantage**

<u>The Golden Apple</u>

Nadji:

"Is the iPhone really the best product out there? It certainly has the highest name recognition, largest market share and intense customer loyalty. Apple's most recent earnings report identified iPhone users with 87 percent loyalty, many of whom pre-order the new version even though their current model is barely worn and working well for them. Word of mouth drives more and more customers to the conclusion that they need to buy the same product leading to nearly insane sales volume (74.5 million new iPhones sold in the fourth quarter of last year). Apple has significantly reduced its marketing and advertising budgets for new model rollouts. The media does the job for the company."

What does this mean for other businesses? Your brand will sell itself if your customers love you, your products and services. Your competitors will have to start knocking off what you are doing to even stay in the game.

*Taking Your Customer Care™ to the Next Level*

<u>Hot Chipotle</u>

Steve:

"The first time I visited what I perceived as an ordinary take out burrito shop at the prompting of my young daughters, I was shocked at the prices listed...$7 for chicken, rice, beans and lettuce wrapped in a tortilla...and I pay extra for chips and salsa! The lines were long and I was tempted to turn around and head down to the little mom and pop Mexican restaurant we usually visited. Well we stayed, the food was good and we return now more than I care to say with our teenage girls. How does Chipotle promote such intense loyalty? Millennials love the brand, its socially conscious approach to ingredient sourcing, and the complete customization of the product. My food is prepared in my clear view exactly as I demand. The taste, smell, sounds, environment and friendly experience are consistent. I always get what I expect as the customer."

**Thought Leadership for Brands**

**Harvard Business Review identified five behaviors critical for brands to be recognized as industry thought leaders.**

1. **Pioneering spirit**
2. **Rigor**
3. **Objectivity**
4. **Authenticity**
5. **Clarity**

<u>Southwest Airlines</u>

Micah Solomon illustrated this issue from his experience on Southwest Airlines, as featured in his book, <u>High-Tech, High-Touch Customer Service</u>.

"A dusting of snow left my January flight grounded for a couple hours on the Philadelphia (PHL) tarmac," he wrote. "Not surprisingly, this made me too late for my connection in Denver. So, I stepped off the plane in Denver, thinking I was going to need to wait in an endless line and plead my case for a re-booking, or call the 800 number and wait on endless hold. But immediately, I was met on the jetway by a gate agent from Southwest. She handed me a ticket with my name on it—for the very next available flight to my destination–pulled from a sheaf of already re-booked tickets she was carrying."

Micah goes on to explain: "Southwest realized that more than 99 percent of the people on the late-arriving plane would want to be rebooked on the next flight out of there. And they therefore designed the process to make this happen, without a single passenger even needing to make a request, which is true anticipatory customer service."

## **Invest in Content Marketing: The Art of Organic Selling**

**A recent survey quoted by Inc. magazine stated that 70 percent of consumers want to learn about products through content as opposed to traditional advertising methods.**

### Make Your Business Conspicuous

Companies must stand out from the crowd, which is far easier said than done in the digital world. The goal is to make sure you can be found easily by your current and prospective customers. Creating compelling content is a key driver of awareness. The Internet is very different from the Yellow Pages of old in countless ways. For one thing, naming your business, A-1 Supply Co. no longer puts you at the top of the list. Online marketing requires getting on the radar of Internet "bots" which gather information from websites, perform analysis through complex algorithms developed by the search engines, which by design seek to find the highest quality content for users. Companies like Google are very good at what they do, so there's no effective way to fool them. You can only win by creating consistent and relevant content, reinforced with legitimately obtained backlinks.

Mike Grehan, CMO and managing director at Acronym Media, says: "Audience intelligence, the real 'big data' in the marketing world, is the fuel that will power what is referred to as the 'intention economy.' The more we understand the end user (and the more they understand us, the marketer), the more relevant (and therefore more useful) we become to each other."

"Doc Searls states in the book he co-authored, *The Intention Economy*, 'this new economy will outperform the attention economy that has shaped marketing and sales since the dawn of advertising. Customer intentions, well expressed and understood, will improve marketing and sales, because both will work with better information, and both will be spared the cost and effort wasted on guesses about what customers might want. The Intention Economy grows around buyers, not sellers. It leverages the simple fact that buyers are the first source of money, and that they come ready-made."

**"You don't need advertising to make them… The Intention Economy is about buyers finding sellers, not sellers finding (or 'capturing') buyers." – Doc Searls**

**Fans are Important Whether they are Purchasers or Not**

Many companies focus all their content creation, care and attention on converting customers yet miss the boat on engaging with fans that may or may not ever purchase from you. Rand Fishkin, CEO and founder of Moz, stated: "The greatest myth is that people absorb brand content and then immediately go to purchase a product. Instead, the path of content marketing is slow and winding, and it may never end in a conversion."

We all know that sales are essential. Without paying customers, businesses would cease to exist. But your most vocal advocates are selling your business for you. They are just as important as those who are purchasing regularly and should be recipients of your affection. Fans are powerful sources of word of mouth marketing that bring paying customers straight to you.

## Word of Mouth

Michael Stelzner of Social Media Examiner interviewed Ted Wright, founder and CEO of Fizz. Wright defines word-of-mouth marketing as "identifying your influencers and coming up with a story that is interesting, relevant and authentic that ladders back to qualities of your brand and then sharing that story as much as possible."

That's the first part. The second part, Wright says, is "creating for your influencers as many opportunities as you can as a brand or a company for them if they feel like it to share your brand's story with as many people as they would like to do so."

Wright identifies the three critical components of a story being shared:

1. Is the story interesting to influencers so they will pick it up, study it and really understand it?
2. Is it relevant to influencers' audiences?
3. Is it authentic the way they currently understand the brand and the category in general?

## Be Creative

Test and trial new initiatives for Customer Care™ to continue raising the bar, going up the ladder, and *Taking Your Customer Care™ to the Next Level*.

# Create a Competitive Advantage with *Next Level Customer Care*™

In this manner you cannot maintain appropriate customer retention.

# SUMMARY

## The Skill that Delivers Awesome Customer Care™: Taking Responsibility

Alexis Ternoy of EPAM shared the story of a customer who had ordered food delivery but after it was all arranged, was not able to be home to receive it. When contacted by a customer service representative, he explained that his wife was in the hospital with an infection caused by her treatment and that he had completely forgotten about the order. The customer service representative he talked to arranged for redelivery for the food order at a later date. But he could not believe it when the delivery man came to the door. Not only did he receive his food order, but they also delivered a large bouquet of flowers for his wife. He said that they could not have timed it better as they had only been home half an hour after being finally discharged from the hospital.

Now that is *Taking Your Customer Care™ to the Next Level*. Clearly someone took responsibility, accountability. Someone took charge of *Going the Extra Mile*.

**To Take Your Customer Care™ to the Next Level, You must go above and beyond. You Must Go the Extra Mile!**

## The Era of the Customer

We have clearly entered The Era of the Customer. With intensifying competition and ever-increasing customer demands, a company will live or die by the level of care and service they provide.

The American Marketing Association is leading a focus on the 2020 Customer. AMA presents the New Four A's of Marketing along with Hillary Ashton, Head of Customer Analytics for Manthan. They outline the path to success now and into the future.

1. **Agility: Get Comfortable with Disruption and Change**
2. **Accountability: Measure the Outcomes**
3. **Appropriateness: Understand your Customer and Personalize their Experience**
4. **Advanced Analytics: Leverage Insights to Engage Customers**

**'On-Demand' Customer Expectations**

Emerging technologies are poised to radically transform the consumer experience, in real time and almost everywhere. According to McKinsey & Company: "The consumer experience (will likely be) integrated across the physical and virtual environment. Most of the technologies needed to make this scenario happen are available now.

- Near-Field Communication
  Embedded chips in phones exchange data on contact with objects that have NFC tags. The price of such tags is as low as 15 cents, and new research could make them even cheaper, so more companies could build them into almost any device, generating a massive expansion of new interactive experiences.

- HTML5 Web Language
  Better-designed online spaces will be created with the powerful new HTML5 Web language.
- Advances in Handling Big Data

McKinsey reports: "Consumers may soon be able to search by image, voice, and gesture; automatically participate with others by taking pictures or making transactions; and discover new opportunities with devices that augment reality in their field of vision (think Google glasses)."

## Better Customer Experience Yields Bottom-Line Results

So perhaps you are one of those people who need to see the cold hard data to prove that investments in improving the Customer Care™ experience will produce ROI.

Forrester Research examined the correlation between additional purchasing, churn reduction and word-of-mouth recommendations across a variety of industries. The research found for example, a wireless service provider with 82 million customers could see as much as $1.6 billion in revenue from additional purchases as a result of improved customer experience. That same company would also experience churn reduction and an increase in word-of-mouth recommendations as a result.

## Differentiation: Avoid the Commodity Trap

Providing *Next Level Customer Care™* is a tangible way to differentiate your business from the competition. Escaping from the commodity trap today is essential in maintaining price integrity. Convince customers that your solutions are sufficiently different from your competition to help you avoid difficult price comparisons. According to McKinsey and Company, a 1 percent change in discounting has a 9 percent impact on your operating margins. A seemingly small price differential can have a significant impact on your company's bottom line.

*Nadji Tehrani; Steve Brubaker*

**Leave the Light on For Customers**

You are probably familiar with budget chain Motel 6 and its spokesperson ending advertisements with "I'm Tom Bodett for Motel 6, and we'll leave the light on for you."

The philosophy is universal that customers want to know you are thinking about them and care enough to make sure they are taken care of in the appropriate context.

Jaimy Ford of Practical Business Training explains: "It's often the littlest things that can make or break a customer experience. Offering a cheery 'Hello' when a customer enters your store. Sending a thank-you note to customers for doing business with your organization. Making customers aware of a perk or discount available to them. Leaving the light on for a family you know is going to show up after dark. Those are all ways to improve the customer experience."

**The bottom line is that in order to *Take Your Customer Care*™ *to the Next Level*, you must *Go the Extra Mile!***

Book Preview - Announcing the Important Follow-Up Book also by the same authors, Nadji Tehrani and Steve Brubaker:

# Taking Your Marketing Strategy to the Next Level™
### Releasing in 2016

**Are You Able to Properly Define "Sales" and "Marketing"?**

Nadji:

""When we hire marketing people at TMC, we give them a marketing test. I have had to 'simplify the test' several times over the years as every college degreed applicant was failing what to me seemed like the simplest of questions. I recall interviewing a Columbia University MBA graduate with 20 years of industry marketing experience."

"He also failed to properly define sales and define marketing"

"Many applicants attributed the same definition to both marketing and sales. They could not distinguish the difference between sales and marketing. I was relieved when finally one of the leading candidates passed my test. So I hired him on the spot and continue to hire based on this important Test for Marketing Ability™.""

*The complete Test for Marketing Ability™ including our step-by-step approach to Attracting, Hiring, Training and Developing Effective Marketing Teams is the subject of the authors' upcoming follow-up to this book:*

## Taking Your Marketing Strategy to the Next Level™

Nadji:

"When I interview someone who tells me they served in the past as a director of sales _AND_ marketing, I immediately suspect they will not succeed in our organization. They have not been educated in the most basic premise of the important differences between the sales and marketing functions. If you hire someone who is knowledgeable about marketing and provide them with support, they will be dedicated and stay with you as your philosophies will align."

## Have you ever wondered why the chief marketing officer is short lived in most organizations?

The average tenure of a CMO is just 45 months, according to a 2014 study released by executive recruiting firm Spencer Stuart. That's nearly double where the average tenure was as recently as 2006, when it was 23 months, but still only half the average time a CEO survives in most companies. In essence, CMO's are being driven out of organizations well before they are able to successfully implement a consistent customer centric strategy.

Suzanne Vranica of The Wall Street Journal interviewed Greg Welch, global consumer goods and services practice leader at Spencer Stuart. Welch said: "Corporations expect chief marketing officers to prove their work has a real impact on driving the business. The CMO chair is a hot seat."

The WSJ reports that although CMO tenure has recently increased, marketing executives are feeling even more pressure to produce immediate results. Companies now "have different expectations of what marketing can do," said John Hayes, chief marketing officer of American Express. "There is an expectation that it's more measurable, more targeted and therefore more effective. This has made everybody's expectations higher," he added.

Marketers must be comfortable communicating with customers seamlessly across multiple channels and effectively deliver content across a myriad of different devices from tablets to smartphones. Big data has produced a tsunami-like effect on businesses as well, meaning that the rules have changed forever, and today's CMO must evolve or risk becoming extinct. "Unless the CMO demonstrates the value that marketing is delivering and clearly shows the return on investment, the business owner, who is under pressure to deliver numbers, will pull funding," said Raja Rajamannar, MasterCard Worldwide's chief marketing officer. "The CMO could find himself out of the job."

Two basic factors are contributing to CMO churn. First, as we've already stated, those CMO's who do not produce immediate ROI are promptly put out to pasture. And secondly, when a CMO does deliver results, the world is watching and offers pour in from competitors and other businesses.

## Marketing Should Be Defined in Four Simple Words: *Generate Qualified Sales Leads*

Nadji:

"That's it! Now you know why I was so frustrated that so many people with college degrees were missing the most basic understanding of marketing!"

## Sales Should Be Defined, as: *Take the Sales Leads Generated from Marketing and Convert them to Customers*

## Your Company will DIE if you are Not Creating Qualified Leads

Understanding and effectively implementing the basic principles of marketing will differentiate your company. Your customers will be more committed and loyal to your brand and you will be a clear and present danger to your competitors.

*Nadji Tehrani; Steve Brubaker*

**One of the first things short-sighted leaders begin to cut from the budget when facing an economic downturn is marketing.**

<u>This is exactly the opposite strategy business should be implementing in this scenario</u>. In a lean environment, you must reinforce your leadership position, and enhance your marketing and *Customer Care*™ processes to GAIN MARKET SHARE. This is another way you can *Take Your Customer Care*™ *to the Next Level!*

For more detailed information and practical guidance on how to successfully hire and develop your marketing team and implement industry leading marketing strategies, refer to the upcoming book by the authors:

***Taking Your Marketing Strategy to the Next Level*™.**

# About the Authors:

## Nadji Tehrani

The Man Who Made Teleservices and Call Centers America's Biggest Growth Businesses

Chairman & CEO, Technology Marketing Corporation (TMC)

- Executive Group Publisher, CUSTOMER™ and INTERNET TELEPHONY® Magazines
- Chairman and Founder, Global Call Center Outsourcing Summit™
- Owner of the registered trademark for the term, "Telemarketing®"

- Recipient of the National Leadership Award from the National Republican Congressional Committee
- Honorary Co-Chairman, Business Advisory Council from Connecticut selected by Congressman Tom DeLay, majority leader
- 2003 ATA (American Teleservices Association) Hall of Fame Inductee

"Nothing in this world is as powerful as an idea whose time has come."

Nadji Tehrani, by any measurement, is a person driven by powerful ideas. With a deep devotion to originality, he is a visionary who for more than two decades has been able to move powerful new ideas from the laboratory to the marketplace in science, business and industry.

As founder of Technology Marketing Corporation in 1972, he has been publisher of more than a dozen periodicals, books and buyer's guides in the high-tech field, including radiation curing. In so doing, he has established himself as the preeminent spokesman in these important and highly scientific fields.

Since 1982, he has gained even more distinction as the nation's most recognized spokesman for the dynamic teleservices industry. As executive group publisher of CUSTOMER (formerly Telemarketing®) magazine, he is an acknowledged leader in bringing this exciting, multibillion-dollar marketing discipline to the forefront of acceptance in America, as well as other nations around the world. As an industry leader once said, "Nadji has done more for the telemarketing industry than anyone." Among the eminent subscribers of Customer Interaction Solutions magazine, one can find many members of the U.S. Senate and House of Representatives as well as leading universities, such as the Harvard Graduate School of Business.

Telemarketing magazine, which began in 1982, has served as the "bible" in helping companies around the globe, and tens of thousands of people have learned how to increase their sales, deliver superior customer service and build market share like never before possible. The magazine has remained number one in its field since its inception, and is now known as CUSTOMER to better reflect the wide spectrum of businesses it serves, which now includes CRM (customer relationship management), e-sales and e-service.

As a leader in the fast-growing information industry, Nadji Tehrani's educational background is equally impressive. Educated in Europe (Sorbonne: The University of Paris), the Middle East and the United States, Nadji has an undergraduate degree in chemistry and has completed graduate studies in business administration.

Before starting his own company in 1972, Nadji held a number of important research, marketing and management positions at E. I. DuPont, Phillip Morris and Stauffer Chemical.

Although Nadji is multilingual, the language he speaks most fluently is the one that business people all over the world understand—that of increased productivity and enhanced profits through teleservices.

In February 1998, TMC introduced INTERNET TELEPHONY® magazine, the authority on voice, video, fax and data convergence. INTERNET TELEPHONY provides complete coverage of this exciting, emerging technology that will revolutionize communications. The magazine went on to launch its own highly successful show, ITEXPO™, the first of which was held in October 1999.

Nadji is the founder of the Global Call Center Outsourcing Summit™, which is the successor to TBT™ (Telemarketing and Business Communications), the world's original and most comprehensive exhibition and conference for CRM, Internet telephony and contact center industries. Over 150,000 top corporate executives are trained annually through CUSTOMER magazine, INTERNET TELEPHONY magazine, the biannual ITEXPO and the Global Call Center Outsourcing Summit.

Among many of his international achievements, Nadji was once selected as one of America's top 500 corporate executives to visit the Kremlin Palace and exchange views with a distinguished delegation of Russian business executives headed by then-President Mikhail Gorbachev.

In 2003, Nadji Tehrani was inducted to the ATA Hall of Fame. The American Teleservices Association is the only association dedicated to the teleservices industry.

Nadji has spoken worldwide on telemarketing and integrated marketing. Domestically, he has addressed dozens of prestigious organizations, such as Sales & Marketing Executives International, the American Red Cross, the Direct Marketing Association, and the National Convention of the American Telemarketing Association as well as at TMC's own Global Call Center Outsourcing Summit. Internationally, he has spoken in Japan, London, Rotterdam, Paris, Mexico City, Canada, Monte Carlo and Brazil.

Nadji's advice is continually sought by the largest financial institutions on Wall Street and investment bankers for his insight on the industry. He is further consulted by a branch of the Federal Government for assistance in conducting the year 2000 Census through telemarketing. In addition, Nadji has been consulted by the Federal Trade Commission (FTC) on matters pertaining to the telecommunications industry.

Nadji has frequently been interviewed by many prestigious national publications, such as The Wall Street Journal, The New York Times, Chicago Tribune, the Washington Post, Fortune magazine and many other esteemed publications around the country regarding matters concerning the contact center industry, as well as industry statistics. Statistics provided by CUSTOMER™ magazine have frequently appeared in the national press, including the Wall Street Journal, and they are a permanent part of the congressional records pertaining to the preparation of the Telephone Consumer Protection Act law.

Technology Marketing Corporation is regarded worldwide as the only credible source of information on the contact center/CRM industry, with over 1,000 audio training tapes, 10 books, six conventions and a 20-year library of information on the industry. As such, Technology Marketing Corporation is the world's leading source of information on the subject of teleservices, customer service, sales and marketing, CRM and Internet telephony. Technology Marketing Corporation owns the registered trademark for Telemarketing®.

Last, but most important, Nadji relates to people. He has dedicated his business and professional career to the enhancement of ideas that enrich the lives of others. Such is the measure of this man and his ideas. Powerful ideas whose times have come...now and for times yet to be!

## Steve Brubaker

Steve Brubaker is Chief of Staff for InfoCision Management Corporation. In this position, he is responsible for staff-related issues, project details, serving as primary negotiator and managing internal and external communications.

Steve began his career with InfoCision in 1985 as a part-time Communicator while attending The University of Akron. He rose through the ranks of the organization, and is now responsible for implementing InfoCision's important operational processes throughout the company. He serves as InfoCision's spokesperson for media-related news and public relations events, and provides internal updates to make sure important developments are announced and promoted.

Under Steve's direction, InfoCision's department of regulatory compliance leads the assessment of internal controls to ensure compliance with the myriad of federal and state regulations imposed on the contact center industry. Steve is directly involved with legal risk management efforts affecting the business strategies for InfoCision's clients. He and his team cultivate relationships with internal departments to develop, implement and audit controls throughout the corporation.

As a member of the Professional Association for Customer Engagement (PACE), formerly American Teleservices Association (ATA), Direct Marketing Association (DMA), International Customer Service Association (ICSA), Society of Consumer Affairs Professionals (SOCAP), and Sales and Marketing Executives Intl. (SMEI). Steve has worked to encourage other industry leaders to get involved both locally and nationally in promoting ethical business practices. He served on the PACE national board of directors for nearly two decades and is active in the PACE Self-Regulatory Organization (SRO).

Steve is a member of The Salvation Army Advisory Board in Summit County Ohio, Akron Public Schools Business Advisory Council, the Rotary Club of Akron, the Executive Advisory Board for The Taylor Institute for Direct Marketing at The University of Akron, The University of Akron Foundation Board, and is an alumnus of the Leadership Akron program.

Steve has been awarded the PACE Telephone Professional of the Year Award, as well as the Call Center Pioneer Award from *Call Center Magazine*, which honors the significant accomplishments and contributions he has made in the industry. In 2006, He received the Lifetime Achievement Award from Technology Marketing Corporation. In 2007 Steve was honored with a Distinguished Sales & Marketing Award from Sales & Marketing Executives International, and was awarded PACE's highest honor, the prestigious Fulcrum Award in recognition of his extraordinary contributions to the industry.

Steve received the 2012 Simonetti Distinguished Business Alumni Award, which is the highest honor bestowed by the College of Business at The University of Akron, and most recently in 2014 was also honored with the Distinguished Alumni Award by the Honors College at The University of Akron.

*Nadji Tehrani; Steve Brubaker*

As a frequent guest speaker for industry events, Steve has been featured both nationally and internationally. He has been part of the PACE Annual and Legislative Conferences, DMA Conferences, and he was the Keynote Speaker for Worldwide Call Centers, Brazil, to name just a few.

Steve co-authored a chapter on direct marketing ethics in a book titled, *Direct Marketing in Action: Cutting Edge Strategies for Finding and Keeping the Best Customers*, which was honored as a finalist for The American Marketing Association's prestigious Berry Book Award in 2008. He has also contributed to numerous industry trade journals and publications, such as *Customer magazine, Customer Inter@ction Solutions, DM News, DMA Insider, DMA Teleservices Council Newsletter, Fundraising Management,* and *Journal of the American Teleservices Association*.

# Appendix:

# The Ritz-Carlton Gold Standards

In the United States, The Ritz-Carlton Investing Company was established by Albert Keller who bought and franchised the name. In the early 1900s, several hotels in places such as Atlantic City, Boca Raton, Boston, Philadelphia, and Pittsburgh, were known as The Ritz-Carlton. However, by 1940 none of the hotels were operating except The Ritz-Carlton, Boston.

<u>The Ritz-Carlton, Boston revolutionized hospitality in America by creating luxury in a hotel setting.</u> The hotel embodies the finest luxury experience, Yankee ingenuity and Boston social sensibilities. The standards of service, dining and facilities of this Boston landmark served as a benchmark for all future Ritz-Carlton hotels and resorts worldwide.

In 1983, The Ritz-Carlton Hotel Company, LLC was formed. Led by president and founding father, Colgate Holmes, alongside Horst Schulze, the company began to expand, adding new properties across the United States. Within two years, the brand had opened five hotels. This rapid expansion continued, and by the close of 1992, The Ritz-Carlton had expanded to 23 exceptional luxury hotels, earning its first Malcolm Baldridge National Quality Award. In 1998, the success of The Ritz-Carlton Hotel Company had attracted the attention of the hospitality industry, and the brand was purchased by Marriott International. Since this purchase, The Ritz-Carlton has continued to grow, providing exceptional service and genuine care to its guests across the globe

## GOLD STANDARDS

The Gold Standards are the foundation of The Ritz-Carlton Hotel Company. They encompass the values and philosophy by which the Ritz hotels operate and include:

### The Credo

The Ritz-Carlton Hotel is a place where the genuine care and comfort of our guests is our highest mission. We pledge to provide the finest personal service and facilities for our guests who will always enjoy a warm, relaxed, yet refined ambience. The Ritz-Carlton experience enlivens the senses, instills well-being, and fulfills even the unexpressed wishes and needs of our guests.

### Motto

At The Ritz-Carlton Hotel Company, "We are Ladies and Gentlemen serving Ladies and Gentlemen." This motto exemplifies the anticipatory service provided by all staff members.

### Three Steps of Service

1. A warm and sincere greeting. Use the guest's name.
2. Anticipation and fulfillment of each guest's needs.
3. Fond farewell. Give a warm good-bye and use the guest's name.

## Service Values: I Am Proud to be Ritz-Carlton

## The Employee Promise

At The Ritz-Carlton, our Ladies and Gentlemen are the most important resource in our service commitment to our guests. By applying the principles of trust, honesty, respect, integrity and commitment, we nurture and maximize talent to the benefit of each individual and the company. The Ritz-Carlton fosters a work environment where diversity is valued, quality of life is enhanced, individual aspirations are fulfilled, and The Ritz-Carlton Mystique is strengthened.

# The Gary L. and Karen S. Taylor Institute for Direct Marketing

The University of Akron (Ohio)

The Taylor Institute was established to advance best practices and disseminate new direct/interactive marketing knowledge. Taylor Institute programs and initiatives are designed to be integrated with the College of Business Administration Marketing curriculum. This integration helps provide experiential learning opportunities to supplement the theoretical, classroom knowledge gained by students, which truly makes the Taylor Institute a location where "theory meets practice."

"The concept of an institute dedicated to direct marketing gives Karen and I a way to help students and promote direct marketing as a possible career path. It elevates a profession and gives students an opportunity to sample something they otherwise might not consider as a career." – Gary L. Taylor

Taylor Institute Mission

To Develop and Inspire Direct/Interactive Marketing Business Leaders through Education, Research, and Service.

- Education Mission: To develop and strengthen curriculum content, instructional methodologies, and learning experiences within the academic and professionals fields of direct/interactive marketing education.

- Research Mission: To advance and disseminate the knowledge of the theory and practice of direct/interactive marketing through theoretical, applied, and pedagogical research and intellectual endeavors.
- Service Mission: To support and expand the general well-being of the university, professional, and community stakeholders who have a vested interest in the Taylor Institute's initiatives and activities and to promote social responsibility within the greater direct/interactive marketing profession.

Services Available to the Business Community

Research and Analytics Laboratories at the Taylor Institute provide corporate clients with cost-effective marketing research and analysis. This analysis focuses on both qualitative and quantitative research analysis, including:

- Focus group analysis
- In-depth interviews
- Implementation of a company-wide data dictionary
- Survey writing and analysis
- Customer base acquisition
- Customer base cloning
- E-mail marketing and display ads
- Descriptive and predictive analysis
- Usability studies

In addition to this analysis, customized corporate training for marketing research, marketing analytics and web analytics are offered. Finally, thought leadership research (an in-house project) focusing on the way universities communicate to their current and prospective students is in progress.

The Research and Analytics Laboratories, located in the Taylor Institute for Direct Marketing, utilizes its state of the art facilities throughout projects including a Marketing Analytics Lab, Focus

Group Lab, Social Media Lab, the InfoCision Call Center and the Xerox Cross-Media XMPie Lab. With these many resources, the Research and Analytics Laboratories are equipped to facilitate in-depth research from start to finish.

Edwards Brothers Malloy
Oxnard, CA USA
September 2, 2015